COOKING WITH

The Young and the Restless™

COOKING WITH

The Young and the Restless™

ROBERT WALDRON
AND MARTHA HOLLIS

WITH NANCY BRADLEY WIARD

RUTLEDGE HILL PRESS

Nashville, Tennessee

Photographic credits: Special thanks to CBS photographers Monty Brinton, Tony Esparza, Cliff Lipson, Richard Cartwright, Michael Yarish, and G. Overton for allowing their photographs to be reproduced here. Photographs on pages 21, 28, 29, 32, 33, 41, 44, 47 (left), 48, 50, 52, 56, 58, 62, 64, 67, 68, 70, 72, 84, 86, 90, 93, 108, 110, 115, 117, 120, 126, 128, 129 (bottom), 131, 132, 133, 137, 145, 152, 157 (right), 158 (bottom), 159 (top), 160, 161, 165 (right), 170, 171, 174 (left), 183, and 184 by Monty Brinton. Photographs on pages 7, 46, 63 (right), 113 (top), 127, 157 (left), 158 (top), 168, and 175 by Tony Esparza. Photographs on pages 8, 10, 20, 27, 42, 61, 65, 96, 103 (right), 136, 142, 150, 172, and 176 by Cliff Lipson. Photographs on pages 74 and 77 by Richard Cartwright. Photograph on page 155 by Michael Yarish. Photograph on page 166 by G. Overton. Photographs on pages 9, 11, 14, 16, 34, 36, 39, 47 (right), 55, 63, 80, 100, 102, 113 (bottom), 118, 129 (top), 139, 141, 143, 148, 154, 165 (left), 169, 173, 174 (right), 179, 182 (left) by CBS. Photographs on pages 24, 26, 37, 81, 91, 95, 97, 103 (left), 105, 134, 138, 140, 146, 159 (bottom), 162, 164, and 180 by John Pascal/JPI. Photograph on page 30 by Downtown Photo, Nashville, Tennessee. Photographs on pages 167, 181, and 182 (right) by Kathy Hutchins/Hutchins Photo Agency.

Published in Nashville, Tennessee, by Rutledge Hill Press, 211 Seventh Avenue North, Nashville, Tennessee 37219. Distributed in Canada by H. B. Fenn & Co., Ltd., 34 Nixon Road, Bolton, Ontario L7E 1W2. Distributed in Australia by The Five Mile Press Pty. Ltd., 22 Summit Road, Noble Park, Victoria 3174. Distributed in New Zealand by Tandem Press, 2 Rugby Road, Birkenhead, Auckland 10. Distributed in the United Kingdom by Verulam Press, Ltd., 152a Park Street Lane, Park Street, St. Albans, Hertfordshire AL2 2AU.

Design by Gore Studio Inc., Nashville, Tennessee.
Typography by John Wilson, Nashville, Tennessee.

Library of Congress Cataloging-in-Publication Data

Waldron, Robert.
    Cooking with the Young and the restless / Robert Waldron and Martha Hollis.
        p.   cm.
    Includes index.
    ISBN 1-55853-548-9 (hardcover)
    1. Cookery.   2. Young and the restless (Television program).
I. Hollis, Martha.   II. Title.
TX714.W2615   1997
641.5—dc21   97-38173
                                                     CIP

Printed in the United States of America.

1 2 3 4 5 6 7 8 9 — 99 98 97

CONTENTS

INTRODUCTION

A GOLD PLAQUE hangs at the entrance to Stage 43 at CBS Television in Hollywood dedicated to the head writer and executive producer of *The Young and the Restless*, William J. Bell, acknowledging his tremendous contribution to daytime television. The plaque also commemorates the taping of the top-rated serial's five thousandth episode in 1992. Stage 43 is one of two stages where *The Young and the Restless* is taped. Next door, at Stage 41, set-side parties are usually held to celebrate such milestones as show anniversaries, ratings victories, and Mr. Bell's birthday. The food served at the parties rivals the lavish meals depicted on *The Young and the Restless* and features such mouth-watering delights as gourmet cheeses, zesty pasta dishes, exotic seafood specialties, and scrumptious cakes.

Not far from Stage 43 is the CBS commissary, which is usually an early stop for actors in the morning. It's where they can pick up a cup of coffee or a light breakfast before beginning work. The CBS commissary is also where the cast and crew of *The Young and the Restless* enjoy lunch. Lauralee Bell (Chris) favors salads and is usually accompanied by costars Doug Davidson (Paul) and Laura Bryan Birn (Lynne). More often than not, they take their meals in either Lauralee or Doug's dressing room, where they also run lines for the day's script.

When the story line had Ashley Abbott brutally attacked by two thugs while walking through the woods in 1996, Shari Shattuck,

The Young and the Restless' creator William J. Bell celebrates his birthday in 1996 at the studio with his wife, co-creator Lee Phillip Bell. The cake is decorated with a likeness of William J. Bell.

William J. Bell and his wife, Lee, celebrate their forty-second wedding anniversary surrounded by their family (left to right: eldest son Bill Jr.; his wife, Marie; Lee; Bill; daughter Lauralee; Colleen, Bradley's wife; and youngest son Bradley).

who plays Ashley, was a memorable sight in the commissary during the sequences following the attack. In the script it took several weeks for Ashley to recover from her bruises. After visiting the hair and makeup room, Shari frequently headed for the commissary, where the realistic bruises on her face elicited concerned looks from other diners who didn't realize it was only part of her character.

The Young and the Restless' premiere on March 26, 1973, ushered in a new age of daytime drama. Creators William J. Bell and Lee Phillip Bell placed a strong emphasis on the emotional plight of young adults struggling to come of age in a confusing and rapidly changing world. From the first episode, the series dazzled viewers with outstanding production values, contemporary music, and compelling story lines that courageously explored such previously taboo subjects as date rape, alcoholism, and drug abuse.

(continued on page 10)

Bill Bell's Incredible Pot Roast

William J. Bell's workday usually begins promptly at 5 A.M., when he weaves the compelling love stories that have made *The Young and the Restless* America's favorite daytime serial for ten consecutive years. Besides serving as head writer and senior executive producer of the show, he is also story consultant for *The Bold and the Beautiful*, which he created with his wife, Lee. Despite such a tremendous workload, he tries to take time, whenever possible, for a breather. One of the ways he relaxes is over home-cooked meals with his family. He shares his special pot roast recipe below, which is a perennial favorite with his family and friends. The entire process can take as little as 3 hours or as many as 5, depending on whether you can wait that long once you've inhaled the aroma. Guaranteed a sure winner!

4   pounds pot roast
2   packages onion soup mix (4 envelopes)
3   large packages slivered almonds
    Very generous amount of small pimento olives
3   large cans baby peas
4   large cans baby potatoes
1   bottle red wine (good quality)
4   cans sliced water chestnuts

■ Brown meat in a large cooker, searing each side and using a small amount of water to keep from burning. Let simmer 30 minutes. Add 1 envelope onion soup mix, ½ cup water, and ¼ bottle of red wine. Cook over low heat for at least one hour, turning it several times. As it cooks, you may want to add more onion soup mix and water. Continue on low heat for another hour, then add peas, potatoes, another ¼ bottle of red wine, and the remainder of the onion soup mix. During the final 30 minutes sprinkle in sliced water chestnuts, slivered almonds, small pimento olives and remainder of baby peas.

The Newmans are a prominent family on The Young and the Restless. *Here is the extended family during Nick and Sharon's wedding reception in 1996 (back row, left to right: Victoria; her husband, Cole; Nikki; Victor; Sharon, Nick's bride; and Nick; front row: Doris, Sharon's mom; and Miguel, the Newmans' houseman).*

Set in Genoa City, Wisconsin, the show originally centered around the lives of two diverse families, one wealthy (the Brooks) and the other financially strapped (the Fosters). Newspaper publisher Stuart Brooks and his wife, Jennifer, had four daughters: Lauralee, a writer; Leslie, a concert pianist; Chris, a journalist; and Pam, a student. Meanwhile, Liz Foster, who had been abandoned by her alcoholic husband, Bill, worked at Chancellor Industries and struggled to put her oldest son, Snapper, through medical school and her second son, Greg, through law school. Liz's third child, Jill, was a beautician. The two families were drawn together by Snapper and Chris's young romance. During the show's first season, Jill gave up her beautician's job and became a personal assistant to the wealthy Katherine Chancellor, who, like Jill's

father, suffered from alcoholism. When Jill fell in love with Katherine's husband, Phillip, a rift grew between the two women that still exists today, twenty-four years later.

The first restaurant prominently featured on *The Young and the Restless* was Pierre's, owned by Pierre Roland, who frequently treated his customers to musical numbers. Pierre was in love with Sally Maguire, a troubled waitress. Sally, however, loved Snapper and tried to lure him away from Chris. In a misguided attempt to trap him into marriage, Sally became pregnant. When she realized that Snapper was committed to Chris, she stepped aside. Pierre married Sally so that her baby would have a father. Later Pierre was killed during a robbery at the restaurant, and a widowed Sally left town with her infant son.

In 1980 the show's format was expanded to an hour, and shortly after that the focus shifted to two new families: the Abbotts and the Newmans. John Abbott, founder of Jabot Cosmetics, had three children: Jack, a playboy who worked as an executive at his dad's company; Ashley, a chemist for Jabot; and Traci, a teenager who struggled with a weight problem. John's first wife, Dina, abandoned the family, leaving him to raise the children alone. He received much-appreciated assistance from his faithful housekeeper Mamie. Shortly after Abbott married Jill Foster, Dina resurfaced in Genoa City. Eventually, she left to resume the life she had begun for herself in Paris. Meanwhile, business tycoon Victor Newman, a friend of Katherine Chancellor's, fell in love with Nikki Bancroft, a stripper. They married and had two children, Victoria and Nicholas, both of whom went on to work for their father's company, Newman Enterprises. Victoria's marriage to Cole Howard, a writer, and Nicholas's marriage to Sharon Collins continues a long-standing tradition of the show to emphasize young love.

Other prominent young couples include Paul Williams, a private detective, and his wife, Chris, a lawyer. Together, they fight for the rights of underdogs. Jabot executive Neil Winters is married to Drucilla, a top Jabot model. Meanwhile, Neil's brother, Malcolm, a Jabot photographer, is married to Dru's sister, Olivia, a doctor. Victoria Newman Howard's former husband, Ryan McNeil, is also an executive at Jabot and is married to Nina, Chris's best friend, who's also the mother of Phillip, Jill's grandson.

Recently, a new family was introduced—the Dennisons. Businessman Keith Dennison, who's romantically involved with Jill, has two daughters, Tricia and Megan, both students. While Tricia was doing research at Jabot for a school paper, she met and fell in love with Ryan McNeil.

Executive producer Ed Scott, who's been professionally associated for more than twenty years with *The Young and the Restless* in various positions, works closely with William J. Bell to draw on the best creative talent to produce a show that sets the tone for the daytime industry of exquisite production standards and strong storytelling. The highly respected serial has won more than sixty Emmys, including five for Outstanding

The Abbotts have played a critical role in The Young and the Restless *since the early 1980s. From left to right, Jack Abbott, the shrewd businessman and charismatic man about town; Traci Abbott Connelly, best-selling author, happily married to publisher Steve Connelly; Ashley Abbott, the bright and beautiful president of Jabot Cosmetics and creator of Jabot's fabulous fragrances; and John Abbott, the patriarch, founder, and chief executive officer of Jabot Cosmetics.*

Daytime Drama. Other awards include The People's Choice Award for "Favorite Daytime Drama" and the NAACP Image Awards for "Outstanding Daytime Drama." The best proof of the show's unprecedented success, however, can be found in its' popularity with viewers. Since 1988 *The Young and the Restless* has been the number one–rated soap in America. It's also seen in thirty-one countries, including Australia, Barbados, Canada, France, Israel, Uganda, and the United Kingdom.

Whether it's a candlelit dinner for two at the lush Colonnade Room, or an intimate picnic on a tropical Caribbean beach, food has always served as a splendid aphrodisiac to help propel *The Young and the Restless'* intriguing love stories. The writers add notes to the scripts suggesting what foods they envision for a particular scene that includes a meal, such as a dinner Nikki might be hosting at the Newman ranch. Executive producer Edward Scott, working closely with the set decorators, directs a caterer such as Gourmet Propers to prepare the beautifully styled meals seen in the episode.

If the scenes continue over more than one episode, such as a wedding or holiday party, the food is set up again to look exactly the same as the episode that was taped previously. Multitiered wedding cakes usually have a least one layer of actual cake; the rest are Styrofoam. While the episode is being taped, the only time actors actually eat the food is when they're supposed to be eating in the scenes. After the last scene is taped, however, the cast and crew are invited to enjoy the food.

Thirty-nine of the recipes that follow were contributed by thirty-one of the show's actors. They are dispersed throughout the chapters, which are arranged in menu-driven chapters as well as traditional recipe-driven chapters. In addition to the recipes, readers will find numerous sidebars relating odds and ends from the show's story line to the general heading of a chapter, such as insights into Grace Turner in the Recipes for Singles section. In the first four chapters, readers will find some interesting tidbits about the show's four primary restaurants—The Colonnade Room, Gina's Place, Crimson Lights Coffeehouse, and The Lodge—as well as holiday and family celebrations, romantic meals, and marriages and honeymoons directly tied to the show's story line.

You can enjoy these recipes as you reminisce about the show, recalling the tender moments as well as the dastardly deeds that have propelled *The Young and the Restless* to the top of everyone's list of daytime television viewing.

COOKING WITH

The Young and the Restless™

Dinner for Two

LUNCH AT THE COLONNADE ROOM

An exquisite French-style restaurant, The Colonnade Room's regal surroundings, a creative blend of Louis XIV and Louis XVI styles, lend a fairy-tale quality to any moment when romance is in the air. Whether it is a marriage proposal—such as Rex Sterling's to Katherine Chancellor, a wedding—such as Victor Newman and Nikki Reed's, or a reception—such as those prepared for Jack Abbott and Luan Volien or Malcolm and Olivia Winters, the lush elegance of The Colonnade Room imbues each occasion with an unforgettable, intimate stamp. Jack Abbott is particularly fond of The Colonnade's private dining room, exploiting its rich appeal to impress the women in whom he has taken an interest. There's always a cozy table for two at The Colonnade Room.

Savoir Faire

LOBSTER AND SCALLOPS NEWMAN IN
PUFF PASTRY SHELLS

WARM CHEESE PUFFS

COLONNADE ROOM MESCLUN SALAD WITH
TOASTED PIÑON NUTS AND
THYME BALSAMIC VINAIGRETTE

GINGER CROUTONS

COLD CURRIED CHICKEN SALAD

PAN-SEARED THREE PEPPERCORN STEAK
DEGLAZED WITH MERLOT

STRING BEANS WITH WARM SESAME SEED DRESSING

ZINFANDEL-BRAISED RED AND GREEN CABBAGES

FRESH PEACH AND PLUM COMPOTE
MARINATED IN SAUTERNS

The Colonnade Room's plush setting makes it the perfect place for couples in love to enjoy a romantic meal.

LOBSTER AND SCALLOPS NEWMAN IN PUFF PASTRY SHELLS

Some occasions call for delicious decadence and a show-off presentation. For convenience, use frozen puff pastry shells that are baked the same day as serving. Lobster and scallops are enveloped in a death-defying sauce of butter and cream and then laced with sherry. What could be finer than, or just as rich as, the Newman family?

½   pound lobster meat
½   pound bay scallops
3   tablespoons butter
1   tablespoon chopped shallots
2   tablespoons flour
1   cup half-and-half
2   tablespoons sherry

■ Cut lobster into bite-size pieces. Completely drain scallops. In a medium skillet melt butter. Sauté shallots for 2 minutes. Cook lobster and scallops until they just turn opaque. Remove seafood and keep warm. Add flour and stir. Cook over low heat for 5 minutes. Whisk in half-and-half until fully incorporated and smooth and heated through. Add sherry and cook 1 more minute. Return seafood to pan and coat with sauce. Cook until seafood is warmed. Divide among baked pastry shells.
Serves 4.

WARM CHEESE PUFFS

The Colonnade Room created this signature dish from the classic French Pâté a Choux (the base for the cream puffs served baseball-sized, three to an order at the Wisconsin State Fair and pumped full of real whipped cream).

The cheese puffs are made with domestic Wisconsin Parmesan cheese, freshly grated before mixing. Do not even think of using powdered Parmesan in this delicate recipe. The water, butter, oil, salt, and pepper are first brought to a boil. Then the flour is stirred in with a wooden spoon and cooked for about 2 minutes to make a dry paste. Eggs are beaten to create a very sticky mixture, and then the cheese is added. Balls are formed either with a pastry bag or a spoon. To create an airy inside, start with a very hot oven, then reduce the temperature.

1   cup water
2   tablespoons butter
½   teaspoon salt
½   teaspoon cayenne pepper
1   cup flour (bread flour suggested)
3   eggs, beaten
¾   cup freshly grated Parmesan cheese

■ In a medium saucepan bring water, butter, salt, and pepper to a rolling boil. Remove from heat. With a sturdy spoon, stir in all flour. Return to medium heat and cook, constantly stirring, for about 1 minute, until the paste is slightly dry and smooth. Let cool slightly. Whisk in eggs one at a time. The dough will be very sticky and cling to the sides of the pan. Whisk in cheese. Make 1-inch dough balls about 2 inches apart with a small cookie scoop (or use a tablespoon) on 2 well-greased nonstick baking sheets. Bake at 475° for 7 minutes. Reduce heat to 400° and continue baking for 20 more minutes, until the puffs are golden brown. The puffs will be crisp on the outside and sound hollow when baking is completed. Serve warm.
   Note: If a shiny top is desired, just before baking, brush tops with a tablespoon of egg beaten with a tablespoon of water. The dough can be made in advance and frozen.
Makes 60 puffs.

COLONNADE ROOM MESCLUN SALAD WITH TOASTED PIÑON NUTS AND THYME BALSAMIC VINAIGRETTE

The trendiest salads are still the "mesclun mixes"—the lovely assortments of colorful and tasty baby greens. The Colonnade Room delights its guests with this elegant side salad of a leafy stack of the mix, well-dressed with the thyme balsamic vinaigrette. Perfection requires the finest extra virgin olive oil, still green and fruity, balanced with an assertive vinegar such as a balsamic aged in oak. Serve with warm cheese puffs.

9	cups tender, just-picked greens including: red oak leaf, radicchio, arugula, spinach, mache, chervil, lollo rosso, and frisee
⅓	cup toasted piñon (pine) nuts
2	tablespoons balsamic vinegar
2	tablespoons fresh thyme, chopped
1	clove garlic, peeled and pressed or minced
¼	teaspoon salt
⅓	cup extra virgin olive oil Freshly ground pepper

■ Wash greens and spin dry. Toss greens and nuts in a large salad bowl. In a small bowl mix vinegar, thyme, garlic, and salt. Using a fork, whip in olive oil until it begins to thicken slightly. Pour on salad and toss until well-dressed. Divide salad among 6 chilled plates. Sprinkle with freshly ground pepper.

Note: Other fresh herbs that can be used include lemon thyme, oregano, and parsley. Balsamic vinegar originally comes from the city of Modena in the Emilia-Romagna area of Italy. In the sixteenth century this aged vinegar with its concentrated flavors was so precious that it was part of a lady's wedding dowry and was also left in wills. Today in Genoa City, when a couple splits, there is little attention paid to "who gets custody of the vinegar."
Serves 6.

GINGER CROUTONS

It is amazing how just a sprinkle of spice and a toast in the oven can transform a former piece of bread into an exotic garnish.

3	slices day-old bread Vegetable spray
½	teaspoon ground ginger
¼	teaspoon salt
¼	teaspoon ground black pepper

■ Cut bread into ½-inch cubes. Spray baking sheet with vegetable spray. Place bread cubes on tray and spray bread with vegetable spray for about 30 seconds. Sprinkle with ginger, salt, and pepper. Toast at 325°, stirring occasionally, for 20 to 30 minutes or until browned.
Serves 4 as garnish, makes about 1 cup.

COLD CURRIED CHICKEN SALAD

There have been so many ladies' luncheons in Genoa City that chicken salad variations have become legendary. This one uses a spicy dressing of chutney, curry, and yogurt.

3 chicken breasts, boneless, skinless, poached
1 cup plain yogurt
4 tablespoons chutney
1 teaspoon curry powder
1 teaspoon salt
½ teaspoon pepper
2 tablespoons almond slivers, toasted
2 tablespoons raisins
   Romaine lettuce leaves

■ Cut chicken breasts into bite-sized pieces. In a medium bowl combine yogurt, chutney, curry powder, salt, and pepper. With a fork, mix in chicken pieces, almonds, and raisins. Serve on plates lined with lettuce leaves.
Serves 6.

PAN-SEARED, THREE-PEPPERCORN STEAK DEGLAZED WITH MERLOT

When the need for steak hits, Genoa City cognoscenti head for The Colonnade Room for their perfectly aged, hand-cut New York strip steaks. These magnificently rich meats are served with huge steak fries.

1 tablespoon oil
2 New York strip steaks, 8 to 10 ounces each
1 teaspoon salt
1 tablespoon three-color peppercorns, crushed
⅓ cup merlot

■ Heat oil in a very heavy skillet for about 5 minutes. Salt each side of the steak. Coat each side with peppercorns. Cook the first side for 6 minutes. Turn and cook for 4 more minutes for very rare and a single incremental minute for the other favorite degrees of doneness. Remove steaks. Add wine to pan. With a spatula, scrape off all flavor morsels. Cook until reduced by half. Spoon over steaks.
   Note: Add 2 tablespoons heavy cream with wine to the pan for an even richer sauce.
Serves 2 hungry steak lovers.

STRING BEANS WITH WARM SESAME SEED DRESSING

A passel of beans are first cooked and drained. While in their serving dish, the dressing of dark sesame oil and seeds, slightly sweetened, is warmed by the beans.

1   pound fresh string beans
¼   cup rice wine vinegar
2   tablespoons toasted sesame seeds
1   tablespoon dark sesame oil
1   tablespoon sugar
½   teaspoon salt

■ Remove tough ends from beans. Cook beans in a large quantity of boiling water for 7 to 9 minutes until they start to lose their crispness. Drain in a colander. In a small bowl mix vinegar, sesame seeds, oil, sugar, and salt. Immediately toss with beans and serve warm.

Note: Toast seeds in a small, heavy skillet over medium heat for about 8 minutes or until they begin to brown. This greatly enhances their flavor. *Serves 4.*

Keemo toasts his parents, Jack and Luan, at their wedding reception, which was held in The Colonnade Room's private dining room.

ZINFANDEL-BRAISED RED AND GREEN CABBAGES

When the cruciferous vegetables reign supreme, the winter months can be filled with this regal presentation of the affordable cabbage. After releasing the fragrance of the allium family, the herbs, apple, zinfandel, and cabbage are slowly braised on the stovetop until the flavors are melded harmoniously.

2	tablespoons oil
1	large onion, chopped
3	cloves garlic, minced
1	small head red cabbage, wedged
1	small head green cabbage, wedged
1	Granny Smith apple, chopped
1½	cups zinfandel (or other full-bodied red wine)
2	tablespoons sugar
1	teaspoon salt
1	teaspoon crushed tarragon

■ Heat oil in a 3-quart pan. Sauté onion and garlic for 2 minutes. Add cabbages, apple, zinfandel, sugar, salt, and tarragon. Cover. Over medium heat cook for 20 minutes or until the cabbage is limp. Cook uncovered for about 15 minutes more to reduce the liquid.
Serves 6.

FRESH PEACH AND PLUM COMPOTE MARINATED IN SAUTERNES

The fruits of summer languish in sauternes to guarantee palate pleasures.

4	large, fragrantly ripe peaches, peeled and pitted
2	plums, peeled and pitted
1	cup sauternes

■ Slice peaches and plums. Place in a glass dish. Cover with sauternes. Refrigerate for at least 1 hour. Serve in a fine crystal glass.
Serves 4.

The Colonnade Room is a favorite of Jack Abbott's, who lost his most recent love, Diane Jenkins, to rival Victor Newman.

GINA'S PLACE

No restaurant in Genoa City has had as diverse a background as Gina's Place. Originally known as Pierre's—named after an owner who was tragically killed during a robbery—it was acquired by renowned concert pianist Leslie Brooks and renamed The Allegro, but running a restaurant interfered with her performances, and she sold it to Jonas. He, however, had more of an interest in Leslie than The Allegro, and when it became apparent to him that his love was unrequited he sold the restaurant to Gina Roma.

Gina's Place is an upscale, family-run Italian restaurant. The dining area is traditionally decorated with matching tablecloths and draperies. The menu includes many authentic dishes, all of which were handed down through Gina's family. In addition to the cuisine, the restaurant has a small stage and a lengthy history of performers. Gina herself has sung for her customers, and occasionally her brother, Danny Romalotti, a pop star, appears as a surprise performer. In earlier days Danny worked as a waiter at Jonas's restaurant, as did Paul Williams.

Specialties of the House

Antipasto Salad

Crostini with Two-Cheese Pesto

Penne Puttanesca

Pasta Primavera

Italian Herbed Chickpea Dip

Roasted Heads of Garlic

Monogram Focaccia

Jeanne Cooper's Sour Cream Baked Chicken

Jennifer Gareis's Spaghetti and Meatballs

Oven-Broiled Salmon Fillets with Ricotta Tarragon Tomato Sauce on a Bed of Wilted Baby Spinach

Sandra Nelson's Warm Linguine with Herb and Caper Sauce

Fettuccine with Portabello and Button Mushrooms

Mushroom Lasagna Florentine

Zucchini Frittata

Tricia Cast's Old-fashioned Beef Lasagna

Grated Zucchini with Onions and Fresh Parmesan Cheese

Orecchiette with Ricotta and Parmesan

J. Eddie Peck's Italian Bread Pudding

Gina's World-Famous Flourless Chocolate Cake

The humble Italian restaurant is a popular lunch spot, becoming one of Chris and Paul's favorites and providing many romantic moments for other couples in Genoa City. It was even a temporary home for Jack Abbott.

ANTIPASTO SALAD

Many of Gina's patrons enjoy this salad as a starter. It is a lively mix of romaine and arugula with marinated vegetables, pepperoni, and gorgonzola in an Italian vinaigrette.

SALAD
2   *cups romaine lettuce leaves, torn*
1   *cup arugula leaves*
1   *cup Giardiniera mix, drained (cauliflower, carrots, celery, peppers, onions marinated in vinegar)*
4   *ounces artichoke hearts, marinated in oil, drained*
20 *thin slices pepperoni*
12 *peperoncini (marinated mild Italian peppers)*
12 *Kalamata olives*
4   *ounces Wisconsin-made Gorgonzola cheese, crumbled*

DRESSING
½   *cup olive oil*
2   *tablespoons julienned sun-dried tomatoes marinated in olive oil, drained*
¼   *cup red wine vinegar*
1   *teaspoon oregano, crushed*
½   *teaspoon cracked black pepper*

■ Divide romaine and arugula leaves among 4 chilled salad plates. Arrange marinated vegetables, artichoke hearts, pepperoni slices, peperoncini, and olives on top. Sprinkle with cheese. For dressing use a total of ½ cup olive oil including that saved from draining the sun-dried tomatoes. Mix oil, tomatoes, vinegar, oregano, and black pepper. Pour over individual salads. *Serves 4.*

CROSTINI WITH TWO-CHEESE PESTO

Gina's customers consume tons of these little Italian toasts. They love this lighter-than-usual version of pesto, in which a substantial portion of the typical olive oil is replaced with ricotta cheese. The resulting topping—a beautiful pale shade of green—is easy to spread.

CROSTINI
½   *loaf Italian bread*
2   *tablespoons olive oil*
PESTO
1   *cup packed fresh basil leaves*
2   *cloves garlic*
2   *ounces Parmesan cheese*
2   *tablespoons piñon (pine) nuts*
½   *teaspoon salt*
½   *cup ricotta cheese*
2   *tablespoons olive oil*

■ Diagonally cut bread into ¼-inch slices. Place on baking sheet. Brush with olive oil. Bake at 350° for 10 minutes until toasted. For pesto place basil, garlic, Parmesan cheese, nuts, and salt into food processor bowl. Pulse until smooth. Add ricotta and olive oil. Pulse until smooth, occasionally scraping down the sides of the bowl. Serve toasts with pesto. *Makes about 2 dozen.*

Gina Roma's warm personality and the great food at her restaurant make Gina's a popular spot with her customers, including Grace Turner and Tony Viscardi.

PENNE PUTTANESCA

Many stories abound about how this southern Italian dish got its name. One of the most often repeated ones is that it was the dish made by "ladies of ill-repute" as it was fast enough to whip up between "appointments." In Rome it is made with spaghetti, but in Genoa City the pasta of choice is penne and fresh basil is added.

¼	cup olive oil
8	medium cloves garlic, chopped
1	2-ounce can anchovies, drained
2	cups canned crushed tomatoes with puree
1	bunch fresh basil leaves (about 20), chopped
1	tablespoon red pepper flakes
1	teaspoon black pepper
¼	cup capers, drained
24	pitted Kalamata olives
16	ounces penne pasta, cooked al dente
½	cup grated Romano cheese

■ In a large skillet heat olive oil with garlic. When hot, stir in anchovies. Sauté until the garlic is golden. Add tomatoes, basil, red pepper flakes, and black pepper and stir until heated, about 5 minutes. Stir in capers and olives. Heat for 1 minute. Place drained penne in a large serving dish. Top with sauce and grated cheese. *Serves 6.*

PASTA PRIMAVERA

Gina, forever helping her clients watch their diets, makes this pasta of "springtime" with low-fat evaporated skim milk instead of heavy cream. By using an imported Swiss Gruyére, Gina makes a radical departure from her usual adherence to Wisconsin-made cheeses. The Gruyére, aged about 18 months, has a special flavor that she loves. The vegetables vary according to what is fresh in the market.

2	tablespoons olive oil
1	onion, minced
2	cloves garlic, minced
1	pound mushrooms, sliced
8	ounces fresh asparagus, cut into 1-inch pieces
1	sweet red pepper, chopped
1	6-ounce can low-fat evaporated milk
1	tablespoon cornstarch
1	teaspoon Italian herbs, crushed
½	teaspoon salt
½	teaspoon white pepper
8	ounces cooked fettuccine, drained
½	cup imported Swiss Gruyere
12	cherry tomatoes for garnish

■ In a large skillet heat oil. Sauté onion and garlic until wilted, about 3 minutes. Add mushrooms, asparagus, red pepper. Sauté until just crisp-tender, about 4 minutes. Reduce heat to medium. In a small bowl combine milk, cornstarch, herbs, salt, and white pepper. Pour over vegetables. Stir until the mixtures begins to bubble and thicken. Place pasta in a large serving dish. Cover with vegetable mixture. Sprinkle with cheese. Garnish with cherry tomatoes cut in half. *Serves 4.*

ITALIAN HERBED CHICKPEA DIP

Serve this with crisp pita triangles, crackers, or breads. Add more lemon juice or oil to thin for a fresh vegetable dip.

1	*15-ounce can chickpeas, drained*
2	*tablespoons extra virgin olive oil*
	Juice of 1 lemon
1	*tablespoon chopped fresh oregano*
1	*tablespoon chopped lemon thyme*
1	*teaspoon salt*
½	*teaspoon black pepper*
	Dash cayenne pepper

■ Pulse all ingredients in a food processor until smooth.

Note: If fresh herbs are not available, substitute 2 teaspoons of dried Italian herbs.

Makes about 1¼ cups.

ROASTED HEADS OF GARLIC

A gentle roasting of whole garlic heads results in a sweet, mild, and tender spread for crusty French bread. After roasting, the individual cloves will easily separate and gently squish out of their papery casing directly onto the bread.

8	*giant whole garlic heads*
3	*tablespoons olive oil*
1	*teaspoon ground thyme*
1	*fresh baguette, sliced*

■ Cut off the tops of each head of garlic to just expose the individual cloves. Place in a small baking pan, tops up. Drizzle with mixture of oil and thyme. Bake at 300° for 1 hour or until the cloves are tender. Serve with fresh baguette slices.

Serves 8.

While they were growing up, siblings Danny and Gina relied on each other for support. The strong emotional bond they share continues today.

MONOGRAM FOCACCIA

This dough is particularly suited for forming the initials of a special friend. Present on a large wooden bread board as the meal's edible centerpiece.

1   *package dry yeast*
1¼ *cups warm water, 105° to 115°*
2   *cups all-purpose flour*
1   *cup whole-wheat flour*
1   *teaspoon salt*
2   *tablespoons olive oil*
2   *tablespoons fresh, chopped herbs*
    (oregano, thyme, rosemary)
    Sprinkle of kosher salt

■ In a large mixing bowl sprinkle yeast on warm water. Mix. Stir in flours, salt, oil, and herbs. Knead on a lightly floured breadboard for 10 minutes. Cover and let rise for one hour or until doubled in size. Punch down. Divide into 2 pieces. Form one large initial directly on each greased baking sheet. Sprinkle with kosher salt. Permit to rise 30 minutes. Bake at 350° for 25 minutes or until the bottom begins to brown. *Makes 2 loaves.*

JEANNE COOPER'S SOUR CREAM BAKED CHICKEN

Jeanne says to bathe chicken breast cutlets in sour cream and coat with Italian bread crumbs, cornflakes, or crispy rice cereal. "The sour cream softens the coarseness of the meat and gives it an unusual flavor."

4   *large chicken breasts, skinless*
    and boneless
1   *cup sour cream*
½   *cup Italian bread crumbs, or crushed*
    cornflakes, or crispy rice cereal
1   *teaspoon crushed Italian herbs*
½   *teaspoon salt*
¼   *teaspoon pepper*

■ Pound chicken to a uniform ½-inch thickness. Place in an ovenproof 10-inch round dish sprayed with vegetable oil. Spoon sour cream over chicken. In a small dish mix crumbs (or cereal) with herbs, salt, and pepper. Sprinkle crumb mixture over sour cream. Bake at 350° for 20 minutes until thoroughly cooked. *Serves 4.*

JENNIFER GAREIS'S SPAGHETTI AND MEATBALLS

MEATBALLS
1   pound lean ground round beef
1   egg
1   slice bread, soaked in water
    and squeezed
1   tablespoon Parmesan cheese
½   teaspoon garlic salt
2   tablespoons olive oil

SAUCE
2   6-ounce cans tomato paste
1   14-ounce can crushed tomatoes
3   cups water
2   tablespoons sugar
2   tablespoons Parmesan cheese
2   tablespoons chopped fresh basil
1   teaspoon garlic salt
½   pound spaghetti, cooked al dente

■ Lightly mix beef, egg, bread, cheese, and garlic salt. Form into meatballs. Brown in olive oil in a large skillet. For sauce mix tomato paste and tomatoes with water in a 3-quart saucepan. Stir in sugar, cheese, basil, and garlic salt. Cook over low heat for 30 minutes. Add meatballs and let simmer for 1 hour. Serve on pasta.
Serves 4.

OVEN-BROILED SALMON FILLETS WITH RICOTTA TARRAGON TOMATO SAUCE ON A BED OF WILTED BABY SPINACH

Salmon, a rich fish, requires little extra fat. After broiling, the fillets are topped with a ricotta-based sauce with French tarragon and fresh roma tomatoes. Dark green, sweet baby spinach leaves catch the drippings from the fish and sauce to round out this presentation.

4   salmon fillets (about 6 ounces each)
1   cup ricotta cheese
4   tablespoons white wine vinegar
2   tablespoons chopped fresh French
    tarragon (1½ teaspoons dried)
1   teaspoon salt
6   Roma tomatoes, seeded, minced
1   pound baby spinach leaves, washed
    Tarragon sprigs for garnish

■ Broil salmon for several minutes on each side. Remove bones and skin. In a small saucepan heat ricotta cheese, vinegar, tarragon, salt, and tomatoes. Place spinach in a large skillet with just the water clinging from its washing. Heat until steam begins to appear. Cover for 2 minutes or until the leaves just begin to wilt. Divide spinach among 4 plates. Place salmon fillets on top. Smother with warm sauce. Garnish with tarragon sprigs.
Serves 4.

SANDRA NELSON'S WARM LINGUINE WITH HERB AND CAPER SAUCE

Sandra shared a handy measurement for dried linguine. Take a fistful of linguine, about the diameter of a quarter. That is about 4 ounces of pasta, which will make about 2 cups of cooked pasta. This recipe, which serves 4, uses 2 fistfuls of pasta, or 8 ounces. She suggests serving with the refreshing Chopped Cucumber and Tomato Salad (page 102).

2   quarts water
8   ounces linguine (or two of Sandra's "fistfuls")
4   tablespoons olive oil
4   cloves garlic, finely minced
1   can anchovies in olive oil
2   tablespoons capers, drained
1   cup chopped fresh basil leaves
1   cup chopped fresh Italian parsley
¼   cup grated fresh Romano cheese

■ Bring water to a rolling boil. Add pasta. Cook until al dente, about 10 minutes. In a skillet heat olive oil. Sauté garlic until soft, about 4 minutes. Add anchovies and capers, stirring until heated, about 2 minutes. Stir in basil and parsley. Heat for 2 more minutes. In a large serving bowl, toss drained, hot linguine with sauce. Top with Romano cheese.

Note: Pulsing the fresh herbs briefly in a food processor speeds preparation time. Be careful to use a light hand and not turn the herbs into a mush.
Serves 4.

FETTUCCINE WITH PORTABELLO AND BUTTON MUSHROOMS

At Gina's this is another popular entrée, especially when she uses the huge portabello mushrooms sliced thick. When served, the customers always think that the portabellos are pretending to be steak without all the negative connotations.

¼   cup olive oil
2   cloves garlic, pressed
2   portabello mushrooms, cleaned and thickly sliced
½   pound white (button) mushrooms, cleaned and thickly sliced
½   cup dry white wine
1   teaspoon salt
¼   teaspoon pepper
1   pound fettuccine, cooked al dente and drained
2   tablespoons chopped fresh parsley

■ In a large skillet heat olive oil. Add garlic. Add portabello and white mushrooms. Cook over medium heat for 8 minutes or until the mushrooms start to soften and release their juices. Add wine and cook until most of the liquid is reduced. Stir in salt and pepper. In a large bowl, toss pasta with mushroom sauce and fresh parsley.
Serves 4 to 6.

MUSHROOM LASAGNA FLORENTINE

With a light mushroom-tomato sauce and a spinach-ricotta layer, this is a light, colorful, and nutritious lasagna. Phyllis sometimes worries that she puts in too much mozzarella for Danny, but that has never happened. Why does Phyllis worry about little things like cholesterol and not big things like paternity and fires?

1   tablespoon olive oil
2   cloves garlic, pressed

1   pound brown cremini Italian mushrooms, sliced (or substitute white button mushrooms)
1   14-ounce can diced tomatoes in puree
½   cup dry red wine
2   teaspoons Italian herbs, crushed
1   teaspoon salt
1   teaspoon crushed red pepper flakes
2   teaspoons fennel seeds
1   pound lasagna noodles
2   10-ounce packages frozen chopped spinach
16 ounces ricotta cheese
2   cups grated mozzarella cheese
1   cup grated sharp provolone or Parmesan

■ Heat oil in a large, nonstick skillet. Sauté garlic for 2 minutes. Add mushrooms, tomatoes, wine, Italian herbs, salt, pepper flakes, and fennel seeds. Cook until mushrooms are softened and the sauce is reduced, about 30 minutes. Cook noodles according to package directions. Plunge into cold water, then drain. Open the tops of the spinach packages. Microwave for about 6 minutes on high or until defrosted. Squeeze outside of package to eliminate as much juice as possible. Mix spinach with ricotta.

Grease a 13x9x2-inch baking dish with olive oil. Cover with a layer of noodles placed lengthwise. Cover with half the mushroom sauce. Place a layer of noodles crosswise. Cover with the spinach mix and ⅔ of the mozzarella. Place a layer of noodles lengthwise. Cover with remaining mushroom sauce. Top with rest of mozzarella and the provolone or Parmesan. Bake at 350° for 40 to 45 minutes. The cheese will be bubbly and begin to brown on top. If the top begins to get too brown, cover with aluminum foil. Let stand for about 10 minutes before cutting into 8 pieces.

Note: Cremini mushrooms are just a bit sweeter than button mushrooms and lose less liquid during the cooking process.

Note: Wisconsin cheesemaker BelGioioso in the town of Denmark (a country drive from Genoa City), is winning natural-cheese championships with its aged, sharp provolone made from cow's milk.

Serves 8.

ZUCCHINI FRITTATA

This little Italian omelet can be whipped up in fewer than 10 minutes. The frittata is a delightful brunch item, especially when served with beautiful red tomatoes.

1	tablespoon olive oil
2	small zucchini, thinly sliced
1	clove garlic, pressed
4	eggs
1	teaspoon Italian herbs, crushed
½	teaspoon salt
¼	teaspoon cayenne pepper, optional
2	tablespoons grated mozzarella cheese
2	tablespoons freshly grated Parmesan cheese

■ In a medium, nonstick skillet heat oil. Add zucchini and garlic. Cook until just wilted. In a small bowl beat eggs with herbs, salt, and optional cayenne pepper. Pour over zucchini mixture and cook until the mixture sets, about 5 minutes. Sprinkle with cheeses. Cover and cook 2 more minutes. Cut into wedges and serve. *Serves 2.*

TRICIA CAST'S OLD-FASHIONED BEEF LASAGNA

Tricia Cast loves old fashioned, traditional lasagnas richly loaded with cheeses. This is a good recipe for a crowd with the advantage of being prepared in advance then reheated. Extra portions also freeze well and will successfully survive microwaving.

SAUCE

1	tablespoon olive oil
2	cloves garlic, minced
1	large onion, diced
1	pound lean ground beef (such as ground round steak)
1	10-ounce can diced tomatoes in puree
1	can tomato paste
½	cup red wine
1	tablespoon crushed, dried Italian herbs
1	teaspoon salt
1	teaspoon ground black pepper
1	tablespoon hot pepper flakes, optional

NOODLES

8   ounces dried lasagna noodles

CHEESE

8	ounces ricotta cheese
6	ounces mozzarella cheese, shredded
4	ounces freshly shredded Parmesan cheese, divided

■ Heat oil in a large skillet. Sauté garlic and onion for about 2 minutes. Add beef. Stir, breaking up into pieces, until meat is browned. Add tomatoes, tomato paste, red wine, herbs, salt, pepper, and optional red pepper flakes. Simmer uncovered until a rich, thick sauce consistency is reached, about 1 hour.

Cook pasta according to package directions. Pour into a colander. Rinse with cold water and completely drain. In a medium bowl mix ricotta, mozzarella, and ½ the Parmesan cheese.

To assemble, spread a small amount of tomato meat sauce on the bottom of a 13x9x3-inch pan. Add a layer of pasta. Cover with ⅓ of the cheese mixture followed by a layer of meat sauce. Repeat procedure with 2 more layers of pasta, cheese, and sauce. Sprinkle top layer with the remaining half of the Parmesan cheese. Bake at 350° until hot and bubbly, about 45 minutes. Let sit for a brief period until lasagna is firm enough to slice.
Serves 8.

GRATED ZUCCHINI WITH ONIONS AND FRESH PARMESAN CHEESE

Sautéed zucchini is quite unlike mushy, boiled, or steamed zucchini. But to achieve this texture, the moisture from the grated squash must first be drained. A handy weighting technique is to place the grated zucchini in a colander with a plate on top holding a 1-pound weight.

1½	pounds zucchini, grated (using large holes of grater)
1	medium onion, minced
2	tablespoons olive oil
3	tablespoons freshly grated Parmesan cheese

■ Drain zucchini and onion in colander for 20 minutes. Heat oil in a heavy, nonstick pan. Sauté vegetables for 5 minutes over high heat or until tender-crisp. Sprinkle with cheese.
Serves 4.

ORECCHIETTE WITH RICOTTA AND PARMESAN

Boiling water for the orecchiette is the only cooking required in this recipe. The remaining ingredients are mixed in a large serving bowl to which the hot, drained pasta is added. The success of this dish is dependent on good-quality, freshly grated Parmesan. Do not even consider making this with the powdered cheese that comes in the cylindrical box. The name of the pasta means "little ears," and this recipe is so easy the cook still has time to hear all the gossip instead of spending time in the kitchen.

> ¾ *pound orecchiette pasta*
> 1 *cup ricotta cheese*
> ½ *cup milk*
> ⅓ *cup freshly grated Parmesan cheese*
> 3 *tablespoons chopped fresh oregano*
> ½ *teaspoon salt*
> ¼ *teaspoon coarsely ground black pepper*

■ Cook pasta in a large quantity of boiling water until al dente. Drain. In a large serving bowl mix ricotta, milk, Parmesan, oregano, salt, and pepper. Toss pasta with the cheese sauce. Serve immediately.

Note: For variety, add chopped black olives, chopped scallions, or sun-dried tomatoes.
Serves 4.

J. EDDIE PECK'S ITALIAN BREAD PUDDING

> 5 *cups cinnamon raisin bread, cubed*
> 5 *eggs*
> 1 *cup sugar*
> 1 *quart milk*
> 3 *tablespoons rum*
> *Whipped cream for topping*

■ Spray a 9x12x3-inch glass baking pan with vegetable oil. Arrange bread cubes in pan. Beat eggs with sugar. Beat in milk and rum. Pour the liquid mixture over the bread cubes. Let sit for 15 minutes to allow the bread to soak. Bake at 325° until the top is lightly browned, about 50 minutes. Serve warm with whipped cream.
Serves 8.

GINA'S WORLD-FAMOUS FLOURLESS CHOCOLATE CAKE

Decadently rich with semisweet chocolate, whole eggs, and sweet butter, this is the dark, sensual cake Gina embellishes for her favorite customers with French vanilla ice cream.

1	*pound semisweet chocolate*
4	*ounces sweet butter*
8	*egg yolks*
1	*cup sugar*
1	*teaspoon vanilla*
½	*cup brewed espresso, room temperature (or substitute strong coffee)*
8	*egg whites*
	Confectioners' sugar for dusting

■ Melt chocolate and butter in microwave or over a double boiler. Let cool. With an electric mixer beat egg yolks gradually, adding sugar until the mixture becomes pale yellow, about 4 minutes. Mix in vanilla. Fold in cooled chocolate and butter. In a separate bowl whip egg whites until stiff, not dry. Fold egg whites into the chocolate mixture. Pour into 2 9-inch cake pans lined with parchment paper and buttered. Bake at 350° in a bain-marie for about 1 hour or until the cake is set. Let completely cool before serving. Dust with confectioners' sugar.

Note: To make a bain-marie, place each cake tin into a larger pan and fill with hot water halfway up the sides of the cake pan.
Makes 2 (9-inch) cakes.

Danny Romalotti and his sister, Gina Roma, both possess a wonderful musical ability and often treat customers at Gina's restaurant with surprise performances.

CRIMSON LIGHTS COFFEEHOUSE

*C*onvenient to Genoa City University and the high school, this is a favorite hangout for the younger set. Abstract paintings, flashy electronic gadgets in nooks and crannies, mission-style chairs, and a jukebox combine to create a hip 1990s coffeehouse crossed with a 1950s-style malt shop. Several relationships have had their start here, including Sharon Collins and Nick Newman. At the time Sharon was dating Matt Clark, a high-school star football player, and her best friend, Amy Wilson, had eyes for Nick. Eventually, Sharon ended her relationship with Matt, and she and Nick began dating, usually ending up at the Crimson Lights. Matt taunted Nick out of jealousy. One night he went too far, claiming he had slept with Sharon, and a fight ensued. Matt won the fight, but Nick won the girl.

Several characters have found a brief haven at the Crimson Lights, including Sharon's friend, Grace Turner. While Grace was laid off from her job at Jabot Cosmetics, she worked as a waitress at Crimson Lights—taking notes as well as taking orders.

Nick's sister, Victoria, also found romantic intrigue at the Crimson Lights. Feeling ignored by her busy husband, Cole, she frequented the coffeehouse to be around others. She flirted with Tony Viscardi and delighted in making Grace, Tony's former girlfriend, jealous. Victoria's former husband, Ryan McNeil, is also a regular diner at the Crimson Lights, occasionally accompanied by Tricia Dennison, who hopes to make her involvement with Ryan permanent.

Crimson Classics

ICED MOCHA

FRESH SQUEEZED ORANGE JUICE

NUTMEG-SUGARED GRAPEFRUIT HALVES

APPLE-YOGURT PECAN MUFFINS

LEMON CURRANT SCONES

JERRY DOUGLAS'S COTTAGE CHEESE PANCAKES

SOFT WHOLE-WHEAT BREAD STICKS WITH RASPBERRY BUTTER

SUN-RIPENED FRUITS AND ALMOND OAT BARS

ORANGE-DATE-WALNUT OATMEAL QUICK BREAD

BRYANT JONES'S CHEESEBURGER NOT DRESSED UP

BAGELS WITH FLAVORED SPREADS

TURKEY SAUSAGE WITH MAPLE BISCUITS

CHOCOLATE BANANA SORBET SMOOTHIE

In addition to being a place where students can hang out, Crimson Lights is the scene of Genoa City University events such as when Nick and Sharon were crowned king and queen of the luau.

ICED MOCHA

Coffee is a treat any time of the day. Served chilled with a hint of vanilla, this iced mocha is a refreshing indulgence.

4   *cups strong, freshly brewed coffee*
⅓   *cup chocolate syrup*
1   *cup half-and-half*
½   *teaspoon vanilla extract*
    Whipped cream for garnish
    Chocolate shavings for garnish

■ In a two-quart pitcher mix coffee, chocolate syrup, half-and-half, and vanilla extract. Refrigerate for at least one hour before serving. Pour into frosted glasses. Garnish with whipped cream and chocolate shavings.
Serves 6 to 8.

FRESH-SQUEEZED ORANGE JUICE

If the oranges are not perfectly sweet, use a bit of sugar to add what nature forgot.

3   *large Texas or Florida juice*
    oranges, halved
1   *chilled glass*
1   *sprig of mint for garnish*
1   *orange slice for garnish*

■ Using a manual or electric juicer, extract juice from oranges. Pour into a chilled glass. Garnish with a mint sprig and an orange slice.
Serves 1.

NUTMEG-SUGARED GRAPEFRUIT HALVES

This citrus sweetened with brown sugar makes a fast microwave treat that's very low in calories and high in vitamin C. The ruby red grapefruit varieties are often sweeter and juicier.

1   *ruby red grapefruit, halved, sections cut*
2   *teaspoons brown sugar*
2   *pinches ground nutmeg*

■ Place fruit on a microwaveable plate. Sprinkle with sugar. Dust with nutmeg. Microwave for about 2 minutes or until the sugar begins to melt.
Serves 2.

Sharon enjoys a playful moment with Cassie, unaware that Cassie is the daughter she gave up for adoption several years ago.

APPLE-YOGURT PECAN MUFFINS

These have become quite popular with the younger crowd who sip and nosh at the coffee shop. They go well with espresso or Iced Mocha (page 37).

1	cup plain yogurt
¼	cup vegetable oil or melted butter
¼	cup sugar
1	egg
1	apple, cored and diced
2	cups flour
½	teaspoon baking soda
1	teaspoon baking powder
½	teaspoon salt
2	teaspoons cinnamon
½	cup pecan pieces

■ In a medium mixing bowl whisk together yogurt, oil or butter, sugar, and egg. Stir in apple pieces. Add flour, baking soda, baking powder, salt, cinnamon, and pecans. Quickly mix. Pour into greased muffin tins. Bake at 400° for 20 to 25 minutes until the tops are golden.
Makes 12 muffins.

LEMON CURRANT SCONES

These golden wedges bake in 12 minutes. A shortcut, after the quick mixing, is to place dough directly on the greased baking sheet, pat it into a circle, and cut into wedges.

2	cups flour
¼	cup sugar
2	teaspoons baking powder
1	teaspoon salt
½	teaspoon nutmeg
¼	cup butter, room temperature
2	eggs
3 to 4	tablespoons milk
	Juice of 1 lemon
½	cup currants
	Zest of 1 lemon, minced

■ In a large mixing bowl combine flour, sugar, baking powder, salt, and nutmeg. Cut in butter until the mixture is the size of chickpeas. Quickly mix in eggs, milk, lemon juice, currants, and lemon zest. Place dough on a greased baking sheet. Using lightly floured hands, pat into a 10-inch circle. With a knife, cut into 12 wedges. Bake at 425° for 10 to 12 minutes until golden.
Makes 12 scones.

JERRY DOUGLAS'S COTTAGE CHEESE PANCAKES

These pancakes are a rich change from standard ones, plus full of protein and calcium from the cottage cheese. Be careful not to overmix. These should be tender cakes.

1 cup cottage cheese
1 cup sour cream
2 eggs, jumbo
1 cup flour
1 teaspoon baking soda
½ tablespoon sugar, optional
 Mixture of canola oil and butter for frying
 Blueberry or strawberry preserves or applesauce for topping

■ In a medium bowl, mix together cottage cheese, sour cream, and eggs. In a separate bowl combine flour, baking soda, and optional sugar. Add dry ingredients to wet ingredients and mix until just combined. Do not worry about a few lumps. Heat griddle. Coat with a mixture of canola oil and butter. Pour ¼ cup batter on griddle for each cake. When bubbles appear on each cake, flip and finish cooking. Serve with blueberry or strawberry preserves or applesauce. *Serves 4.*

SOFT WHOLE-WHEAT BREAD STICKS WITH RASPBERRY BUTTER

These soft, fat bread sticks make a perfect snack for young and old alike. Served warm, the bread will melt the butter like a dip.

BREAD STICKS
1 package dry yeast
½ cup warm water, 105° to 115°
1 tablespoon sugar
1½ cups all-purpose flour
1½ cups whole-wheat flour
1½ teaspoons salt
½ cup milk
3 tablespoons butter, melted
1 egg, beaten

RASPBERRY BUTTER
2 ounces (½ stick) butter, softened
1 tablespoon seedless raspberry jam

■ Sprinkle yeast over warm water. Stir in sugar. Let sit 5 minutes until bubbly. In a large mixing bowl, mix flours and salt. Stir in yeast mixture, milk, melted butter, and egg. Knead with bread hook or by hand for 5 minutes. Put in a bowl. Cover with plastic wrap. Let rise 1 hour or until doubled in size. Punch down. Transfer to a lightly floured pastry board. Divide into 4 pieces. Roll each into a rectangle. Using a sharp knife, cut dough into 8 pieces. Using both hands, roll each piece into a fat breadstick. Place on greased baking sheets. Let rise for 20 minutes. Bake at 350° for 20 to 25 minutes. In a small mixing bowl, cream butter and raspberry jam together. Serve raspberry butter with warm bread. *Makes 32 bread sticks.*

SUN-RIPENED FRUITS AND ALMOND OAT BARS

These fruit- and nut-packed bars, not too sweet, are a healthy morning food loved by children and adults. In the market, look for the packages of mixed, dried fruit bits that may include raisins, peaches, apricots, and apples. Instead of butter or oil, the bar is "shortened" with a puree of prunes.

½ cup prune butter (recipe below)
2 egg whites
⅓ cup water
¼ cup brown sugar
1 teaspoon almond extract
½ cup flour
2 cups old-fashioned oats
1 teaspoon baking powder
½ teaspoon salt
1 6-ounce package (about 1 cup) dried fruit bits
½ cup chopped almonds

■ In a medium mixing bowl combine prune butter, egg whites, water, brown sugar, and almond extract. Stir in flour, oats, baking powder, and salt. Stir in fruit and almonds. Pour into a greased 8-inch square pan. Bake at 350° for 20 to 25 minutes. Cool in the pan. Remove from baking pan and slice on a cutting board into thin bars.

Note: To make prune butter, in a food processor puree a mounded ½ cup of prunes with 2 tablespoons water. If the prunes are dry, more water may be needed.
Makes 32 bars.

ORANGE-DATE-WALNUT OATMEAL QUICK BREAD

This quick bread has lots of interesting tastes plus much lower fat than traditional baking-powder breads.

⅓ cup vegetable oil
1 egg
⅔ cup sugar
   Juice of 2 oranges (about ⅔ cup)
   Zest of 1 orange, finely minced
1 teaspoon vanilla extract
1¼ cups flour
1 cup quick-cooking oats
1 teaspoon salt
2 teaspoons baking powder
1 cup chopped date pieces
½ cup chopped walnuts

■ In a small mixing bowl combine oil, egg, sugar, orange juice, zest, and vanilla. In a large mixing bowl combine flour, oats, salt, and baking powder. Stir wet ingredients into the dry ones. When just combined, stir in dates and walnuts. Pour into a greased 9x5x3-inch loaf pan. Bake at 350° until a knife inserted into the center comes out clean, about one hour.
Makes 1 loaf.

BRYANT JONES'S CHEESEBURGER NOT DRESSED UP

Bryant, at six, likes cheese on his hamburger and he likes the bun. He does not like it "dressed up" with mustard but says "a pickle is okay." He also likes fries with his burgers.

1   *pound lean ground beef*
1   *teaspoon salt*
½   *teaspoon pepper*
4   *slices American cheese*
4   *hamburger buns*

■ Gently form meat into 4 patties. Season with salt and pepper. Broil about 4 inches from heat for about 10 minutes, turning once. Meat should be cooked medium with no pinkness inside. Cover with slices of American cheese and place on buns. Do not add any stuff.
Makes 4.

BAGELS WITH FLAVORED SPREADS

Christine enjoys sesame seed bagels with her coffee, which she picks up at the coffeehouse. A fruited cream-cheese spread is an added treat.

4   *ounces low-fat cream cheese*
2   *tablespoons apricot preserves*
      (or substitute other flavors)
4   *bagels*

■ Allow cream cheese to soften slightly at room temperature. In a small mixing bowl using a large spoon, cream together the cheese and preserves. Spread on toasted bagel halves.
   Note: Spread can be made in advance and refrigerated until needed. Ingredients can also be quickly combined in the small bowl of a food processor.
Makes about ½ cup.

TURKEY SAUSAGE WITH MAPLE BISCUITS

John often orders these for the Jabot Company's breakfast meetings. His bout with high cholesterol makes him more health conscious. He magnanimously shares his healthy choices with his employees.

SAUSAGE
1	*pound lean, ground turkey*
1	*teaspoon salt*
1	*teaspoon ground sage*
1	*teaspoon black pepper*
¼	*teaspoon cayenne pepper*

BISCUITS
	Biscuits (page 147)
1	*tablespoon maple syrup*

■ With a fork, lightly mix turkey, salt, sage, and black and cayenne peppers. Form into 8 patties. Cook in a nonstick skillet sprayed with vegetable oil over medium-high heat about 6 minutes on each side. The centers should be completely cooked. Follow biscuit recipe, omitting cheese, using vegetable shortening in place of the butter, and adding maple syrup. Form into 8 large biscuits and bake as directed. Let cool for several minutes. Slice horizontally and fill each with a sausage patty.
Makes 8 biscuits.

Nikki and Nick posed together for a prewedding photograph the day Nick married Sharon.

CHOCOLATE BANANA SORBET SMOOTHIE

Filming for *The Young and the Restless* continues from 8 A.M. to 6 P.M. Several actors rely on nonfat chocolate sorbet for an energy boost in the late afternoon.

⅔	*cup nonfat chocolate sorbet*
1	*small banana, peeled*
1	*tablespoon honey*

■ Whip all ingredients in a blender until smooth. Serve in a tall, chilled glass.
Serves 1.

THE LODGE

*L*ike *The Colonnade Room, The Lodge is an upscale restaurant catering to couples inter-ested in rich cuisine and a romantic atmosphere. It was designed to combine a New York flavor with traditional English pub decor. The decor follows a hunting motif, utilizing a great deal of mahogany.*

Victor and Diane Newman dine here often. The Lodge is also a favorite of John Abbott. During his marriage to Jill, they were regular diners. More recently, Tricia Dennison enjoyed the ambiance of The Lodge with her platonic pal Alec's posing as her boyfriend. Tricia chose the restaurant because she knew Ryan McNeil would be there with his friend and work asso-ciate Neil Winters. On earlier occasions Tricia also observed Ryan with Nina when they were still together.

Signature Cuisine

SAFFRON-INFUSED BAY SCALLOP SOUP

CAJUN-SPICE BAKED FLOUNDER FILLETS
WITH TOMATOES AND TEXMATI RICE

DUCK LIVER PÂTÉ WITH GASCON ARMAGNAC PRUNE
ON FRESH BAGUETTES BASE

JESS WALTON'S BEEF STROGANOFF

SHARI SHATTUCK'S ROASTED TOMATOES AND GARLIC

SHARI SHATTUCK'S LAMB CHOPS WITH ROASTED
TOMATOES AND ARUGULA

ROASTED BEETS WITH WALNUT AND ORANGE SAUCE

STEAMED BROCCOLI
IN HORSERADISH SOUR CREAM SAUCE

GRAND MARNIER CHOCOLATE CHIP RICOTTA CAKE
IN COOKIE CRUST

The elegant Lodge restaurant evokes the feeling of an Edwardian hunting club. The walls incorporate mahogany paneling and carved mouldings, and the overall space is brightened with lighting and the use of clear, stained, and mirrored glass.

SAFFRON-INFUSED BAY SCALLOP SOUP

The world's most expensive spice, saffron, infuses its golden magic into this delicate soup, which is swimming with sweet bay scallops. First the stock is infused with the saffron. Then a classic roux of butter and flour, which adds thickness and body to the stock, is made. Just before serving, the fast-cooking scallops are added. Serve with rosemary rolls.

> 4 cups fish or chicken stock
> 10 saffron threads
> ¼ cup butter
> 2 shallots, minced
> ¼ cup flour
> ⅓ cup dry white wine
> 1 teaspoon salt
> ½ teaspoon ground white pepper
> 1 pound bay scallops

■ Bring stock to a boil. Remove from heat. Add saffron. Permit to infuse for about 10 minutes. In a saucepan melt butter. Cook shallots over medium heat until translucent, about 5 minutes. Stir in flour. Cook continuously stirring for about 10 minutes. Gradually whisk roux into the saffron stock. Add wine, salt, and pepper. Let simmer for 5 minutes or until thickened. Add scallops. Cook 3 more minutes until scallops just turn opaque inside. Serve hot.

Note: The quality of this soup is dependent upon the stock. The best is a defatted home-made stock. Canned stocks are acceptable, but be very cautious of excess salt. New on the market are stock bases similar to those used in commercial kitchens. Many produce an excel-lent result with little effort. Again, watch for excess salt. Bouillon cubes are not recommended. Serves 6.

CAJUN-SPICE BAKED FLOUNDER FILLETS WITH TOMATOES AND TEXMATI RICE

Purchase a good-quality Cajun spice mix, such as those brilliantly concocted by Paul Prudhomme, from the market. The flounder is baked in a sauce of tomatoes, vegetables, and the spices, then accompanied with the fragrant Texmati rice.

> 4 flounder fillets, about 1½ pounds
> 1 14-ounce can crushed tomatoes
> in thick puree
> 1 medium onion, thinly sliced
> 1 rib celery, minced
> 2 tablespoons Cajun spice mix
> ½ teaspoon salt
> 2 cups cooked Texmati rice
> (or other aromatic rice variety)

■ In a glass baking dish sprayed with vegetable oil, arrange flounder. In a medium bowl combine tomatoes, onion, celery, spice mix, and salt. Pour on fish. Bake at 400° until the fish is just cooked, 30 to 40 minutes. Serve over rice. Serves 4.

DUCK LIVER PÂTÉ WITH GASCON ARMAGNAC PRUNE ON FRESH BAGUETTES BASE

The southwestern part of France is where many of Genoa City's residents dream of disappearing, especially those who dined at Pierre's Place. Since the restaurant closed the best option is a vacation floating on a luxury barge, such as the *Julia Hoyt*, through this area. Only 2 intimate couples per week can take this perfect romantic escape into one of the world's gastronomic regions. This is the home of duck foie gras, gourmet prunes, and Armagnac. And as is the case throughout France, the bakers issue forth fresh loaves of bread every day except Sunday. But until you can convince a lover and a cherished couple to accompany you on this voyage, enjoy this experience of sensuality at home.

1   *pound duck liver pâté*
½   *cup pitted prunes*
2   *tablespoons Armagnac*
     (or substitute any fruity brandy)
2   *baguettes*

■ Slice pâté into 48 pieces. Bring to room temperature. Make a puree of prunes and Armagnac in a food processor. Slice each baguette into 24 pieces. Smear each bread slice with brandy mixture. Top with pâté slice.
   Note: Ficelle, a skinny baguette, makes a beautiful base for crust lovers, since the ratio of soft center to outside is smaller. If making your own baguettes, simply double the number of loaves and make them skinnier. Remember to add ice cubes to the oven during the first 10 minutes of baking to create humidity, which is the foundation of a crispy crust.
Makes 48 pieces.

JESS WALTON'S BEEF STROGANOFF

Jess says that this is a "hearty meal. I like it in the winter. When I was a kid I used to imagine that I was a Russian princess. I'd be in bed and I'd get under the covers and imagine that I was being spirited across the tundra in a horse-drawn sleigh; it would make me feel cozy and protected. I'd fall asleep. I think that's why I like beef stroganoff."

1   *pound beef top loin or tenderloin*
1   *tablespoon butter*
1   *clove garlic, minced*
1   *small sweet onion, chopped*
¾   *pound mushrooms, sliced*
2   *tablespoons ketchup*
⅓   *cup white wine or dry vermouth*
1   *teaspoon salt*
½   *teaspoon pepper*
1   *cup sour cream*

■ Cut meat across the grain into thin slices. In a large skillet sauté in butter for 2 to 3 minutes or until meat begins to brown. Remove meat. Sauté garlic and onion until wilted, about 3 minutes. Add mushrooms. Cook until tender, about 5 minutes. Stir in ketchup, white wine or vermouth, salt, and pepper. Simmer for 3 minutes. Return beef to pan. Stir in sour cream. Simmer until completely warmed. Serve with rice pilaf or fresh noodles.

Note: It is easier to make thin beef slices if the meat is frozen for 10 minutes before slicing. The Italian cremini brown mushrooms are excellent in this dish as they stay quite firm. Also try other exotic mushrooms. Do not use portabellas—they blacken the sauce. Nonfat sour cream can be successfully substituted. Use about 10 ounces of fresh pasta or 8 ounces of dry pasta.
Serves 4.

Michael frequently met with Phyllis at The Lodge to discuss the divorce suit Danny had filed against her. The restaurant's comfortable setting makes it a perfect place to discuss important matters over a meal.

SHARI SHATTUCK'S ROASTED TOMATOES AND GARLIC

Save the juices accumulated while roasting to use for broth in Shari Shattuck's Lamb Chops with Roasted Tomatoes and Arugula (page 48).

2   *pounds ripe Roma tomatoes, cut in half*
12 *cloves garlic, peeled*
1   *tablespoon olive oil*
1   *teaspoon salt*
½   *teaspoon freshly ground black pepper*
1   *teaspoon crushed thyme*

■ Line a rimmed cookie sheet with parchment paper. Place tomatoes on parchment. Roast at 300° until skins can easily be removed, about 20 minutes. Add garlic cloves to peeled tomatoes on baking sheet. Drizzle with olive oil. Season with salt, pepper, and thyme. Return to oven. As juices accumulate, pour off and reserve. Roast until the tomatoes are dried but not crunchy, 2 to 3 hours.
Serves 4.

SHARI SHATTUCK'S LAMB CHOPS WITH ROASTED TOMATOES AND ARUGULA

Slowly simmering browned lamb chops in broth makes them delightfully tender in this dish—somewhere between a soup and a stew. The garlic and tomatoes are separately roasted (page 47) then added to the meat and broth for 20 minutes along with the fragrant fresh herbs. A whole new flavor dimension comes from the arugula, which is wilted by the broth added to the large soup plates. Serve with crusty, hot bread for soaking up the rich broth.

8   *center-cut lamp chops with round bone*
8   *sprigs fresh rosemary*
     Roasted Tomatoes and Garlic (page 47)
8   *cups chicken stock*
8   *sprigs fresh thyme*
4   *cups arugula*

■ Brown lamb in a Dutch oven or large deep skillet. Add stock and cook over low heat until very tender but not falling apart, about 1½ hours. In the last 20 minutes of cooking time add Roasted Tomatoes and Garlic and fresh herbs. Separate arugula into 4 large soup plates. Add lamb and vegetables. Ladle broth into each bowl.

Note: You may substitute the dry version of sun-dried tomatoes, not the kind packed in olive oil, for the roasted tomatoes. Add garlic cloves directly to the broth.
Serves 4.

ROASTED BEETS WITH WALNUT AND ORANGE SAUCE

The full, natural sweetness of fresh beets is intensified when roasted. Do not be surprised when everyone requests seconds.

1½   *pounds beets*
1   *tablespoon walnut oil*
2   *tablespoons orange juice concentrate*
2   *tablespoons water*
¼   *cup walnut halves*
½   *teaspoon salt*

■ Peel beets and cut in half. Place in a baking dish. Rub with oil. Pour orange juice and water around the beets. Roast at 350° for 40 to 50 minutes or until tender. Toast walnut pieces on a separate pan for 10 minutes. Sprinkle nuts and salt over beets.
Serves 6.

STEAMED BROCCOLI IN HORSERADISH SOUR CREAM SAUCE

Broccoli is one of the best tasting of the cruciferous vegetables and available fresh almost year around. Select heads that are dark green with the bluish tinge. Peel the stems and thinly slice so that their steaming time is the same as the florets.

   1¼ *pounds broccoli, before trimming*
   ½   *cup sour cream*
   2   *teaspoons creamy horseradish*
   ½   *teaspoon salt*
   ¼   *teaspoon ground white pepper*

■ Cut off tough, fibrous end of broccoli. Cut off tops to make individual florets. With a small knife peel stems. Slice into ¼-inch pieces. Steam broccoli until tender-crisp, about 4 minutes. Drain in steamer for several minutes. In a serving dish combine sour cream, horseradish, salt, and pepper. Stir in broccoli.
Serves 4.

GRAND MARNIER CHOCOLATE CHIP RICOTTA CAKE IN COOKIE CRUST

This is a rich and grand dessert. For extra festivity, try it with the Rich Chocolate Fudge Sauce (page 183).

COOKIE CRUST
  1½ *cups chocolate cookies*
  ⅓   *cup ground walnuts*
  ¼   *cup Grand Marnier liqueur*
  3   *tablespoons melted butter*

FILLING
  2   *cups ricotta cheese*
  8   *ounces cream cheese*
  1   *cup sugar*
  3   *eggs*
  ¼   *cup Grand Marnier*
  ½   *teaspoon salt*
  1   *cup mini semisweet chocolate chips*
  2   *tablespoons grated orange zest*
 12   *walnut halves for garnish*

■ Combine chocolate cookies, walnuts, liqueur, and butter in a food processor. Pulse until well combined. Using fingers, press dough into the bottom of a 10-inch springform pan. For filling, place ricotta, cream cheese, sugar, eggs, liqueur, and salt in processor bowl. Pulse until smooth. Stir in chocolate chips and zest. Pour into springform pan. Bake at 325° for 1 hour or until set. Garnish with walnut pieces. Refrigerate overnight before serving.
Serves 12.

Holiday and Family Celebrations

Holidays and celebrations in Genoa City provide perfect opportunities for friends who have lost touch to get reacquainted and for families to enjoy lavish, home-cooked means in intimate surroundings. Certain occasions, such as the Independence Day picnic at the Newman ranch, are annual events. Regardless of the occasion or celebration, one thing is certain: each affair has its own special menu, making it an extraordinary event with style and zing.

NEW YEAR'S EVE AT THE CHANCELLORS'

MICHAEL DAMIAN'S BAY SCALLOP RISOTTO

WARM CHILI-ROASTED PECANS

BACKFIN CRAB CAKES ON SWEET RED PEPPER PUREE

SOUTHERN JAMBALAYA

COUNTRY STYLE GARLIC AND PEPPER-INFUSED BLACK OLIVES

BROOK MARIE BRIDGES'S
CRISPY OVEN-FRIED CHICKEN DRUMSTICKS

CUMIN EGGPLANT DIP WITH PITA TRIANGLES

STEAMED NEW POTATOES WITH DILL MUSTARD DIPPING SAUCE

SAUSAGE TORTELLINI WITH WARM ITALIAN DIPPING SAUCE

FRESH CORN GRIDDLE CAKES WITH AVOCADO CREAM

FETA CHEESE AND BABY SHRIMP PHYLLO TRIANGLES

ROASTED OYSTERS ON THE HALF SHELL WITH
WHITE WORCHESTERSHIRE SAUCE

FRESH MOZZARELLA, AVOCADO, AND
TOASTED SUNFLOWER SEEDS WITH LIME-CILANTRO
SAUCE AND SOURDOUGH TOASTS

When word spread that Katherine was hosting a New Year's party, it created a bit of a stir. The mansion had not seen such an elaborate party since her husband's death. Among the fortunate invitees were Katherine's close friend Nikki and her new husband, Josh. Several members of the Abbott family were also invited, including Jack, his girlfriend Diane, Ashley, and John.

One person not invited was Katherine's longtime nemesis, Jill. Now that Jill was no longer married to John, Katherine felt relieved that she was not obligated to include her in the party plans. As New Year's Eve approached, Jill found that she had no special plans, and hardly being the type to stay home alone, she crashed the party. Although she was not particularly pleased with Jill's being there, Katherine refused to make a scene. When the magic moment arrived, Katherine offered her guests an optimistic midnight toast for the new year.

MICHAEL DAMIAN'S BAY SCALLOP RISOTTO

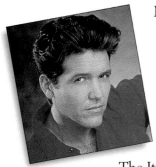

Michael says, "I'm Italian. My family is from Italy. My mother cooks Italian food. My first love is Italian food." In the traditional manner, the aromatic garlic and onions are first sautéed in olive oil. The Italian short-grained rice called arborio is stirred into the oil until each grain is completely coated. Then hot chicken stock is added ½ cup at a time and stirred

until absorbed. The stirring process continues for about 20 minutes until all the stock has been added and absorbed. In this seafood version, fresh bay scallops are added at the end along with Italian parsley, Parmesan cheese, and lemon wedges.

1	tablespoon olive oil
2	cloves garlic, minced
1	small onion, minced
1	cup Arborio rice
8	cups hot chicken stock, divided
1	pound small bay scallops, drained
2	tablespoons chopped, fresh, long-leaf Italian parsley
½	cup freshly shredded Parmesan cheese Lemon wedges for garnish

Jill was determined not to be alone on New Year's Eve and shamelessly crashed Katherine Chancellor's holiday party.

■ In a large skillet heat olive oil. Sauté garlic and onion until limp, about 3 minutes. Stir in rice until all grains are coated with oil. Reduce heat to medium. Add ½ cup of hot stock. Stir until it is absorbed. Continue adding stock ½ cup at a time until absorbed. Total cooking time will be about 20 minutes. Stir in scallops until cooked, about 2 minutes. Transfer to a heated serving platter. Sprinkle with parsley and Parmesan cheese. Garnish with lemon wedges. Serve immediately.
Serves 4.

WARM CHILI-ROASTED PECANS

Be forewarned—these spicy pecans jump right out at unsuspecting people who are trying to ignore them. Double the recipe if you want any left for the guests. Use a heavy skillet and keep a watchful eye as the nuts easily burn.

2	*tablespoons oil*
2	*tablespoons chili powder (as sold in supermarkets mixed with cumin, oregano, salt)*
1	*teaspoon salt*
2	*teaspoons sugar*
1	*teaspoon black pepper*
3	*cups pecan halves, shelled*

■ In a large, heavy skillet combine all ingredients except pecans. Cook over medium heat for 2 minutes or until the fragrance of the spices is released. Stir in nuts. Reduce heat to low. Cook 15 minutes, tossing occasionally and being careful not to burn the nuts. Serve warm.
Makes 3 cups.

BACKFIN CRAB CAKES ON SWEET RED PEPPER PUREE

Crab is one of the most delicate shellfish. To remove the cartilage, spread crab on a baking sheet. Run under the broiler for about 2 minutes. The cartilage will become opaque before the crab begins to cook.

1½	*pounds backfin crabmeat, cleaned of all cartilage and shell*
1	*cup bread crumbs, made from fresh bread*
1	*egg, beaten*
1	*teaspoon Old Bay seasoning*
1	*tablespoon oil*
1	*red bell pepper, seeded and cored*
1	*shallot, minced*
½	*teaspoon thyme*
½	*teaspoon salt*
2	*tablespoons dry white wine*
4	*fresh thyme sprigs*

■ With a fork gently combine crab, bread crumbs, egg, and the Old Bay seasoning. Form into 8 cakes. Cook on an oiled nonstick griddle until each side is golden brown. In a saucepan, steam pepper over 1 inch of water for 8 minutes. Drain water. Puree in a food processor. Return to sauce pan with shallot, thyme, salt, and wine. Reduce until a sauce consistency is reached. To serve, place 2 crab cakes on each plate. Nap with puree and garnish with thyme sprig.
Serves 4.

SOUTHERN JAMBALAYA

While the inspiration for this meal comes from the Louisiana Creoles, the ingredients, particularly the use of turkey sausage and lean chicken breast, are in tune with the current healthier cooking styles. The sausage and chicken are first sautéed, removed from the skillet, and returned near the end of cooking to keep them tender and moist. Since the shrimp cook very rapidly, they appear in the skillet just minutes before serving. Pass with hot sauce made from the famous Tabasco peppers grown on McIlhenny Island.

1	tablespoon vegetable oil
½	pound spicy, Italian turkey sausage, cut into 1-inch slices
1	large chicken breast, cubed
1	large onion, chopped
2	cloves garlic, minced
2	ribs celery, chopped
1½	cups uncooked, long-grain white rice
1	14-ounce can diced tomatoes with liquid
2½	cups chicken stock or water
1	teaspoon salt
1	teaspoon ground thyme
½	teaspoon cayenne pepper
1	pound peeled shrimp

■ In a large skillet with an ovenproof handle heat oil. Sauté sausage and chicken pieces until no longer pink inside, 8 to 10 minutes. Remove meat. Sauté onion, garlic, and celery for 5 minutes. Stir in rice and coat with oil. Add tomatoes, stock or water, salt, thyme, and cayenne. Bring to a boil. Reduce heat to simmer. Cover and cook until the rice is tender, about 15 minutes. Stir in cooked sausage and chicken. Add shrimp. Cook until the shrimp are pink, about 3 minutes. If there is excess liquid, place skillet in a 350° oven to slightly dry out, about 5 minutes.
Serves 6 to 8.

COUNTRY-STYLE GARLIC AND PEPPER-INFUSED BLACK OLIVES

The ordinary California black olive becomes a company food by adding garlic, vinegar, and herbs. By using the pitted variety, the dilemma of what to do with the pit is eliminated. Plan to start these 3 days in advance of serving.

1	7-ounce can California black olives, pitted
½	cup brine from olives
2	cloves garlic, peeled and lightly smashed
½	cup red wine vinegar
1	teaspoon coarse-ground black pepper
1	teaspoon dried oregano

■ Drain olives, reserving ½ cup of brine. Place in a 2-cup glass or plastic container with garlic, red wine vinegar, pepper, and oregano. Shake well. Store refrigerated for at least 3 days before serving.
   Note: For easy peeling, drop garlic cloves into boiling water for 20 seconds. Rinse under cold water. Place on a cutting board and smash with the side of a heavy chef's knife. The skins will slip off easily.
Makes about 1 ½ cups.

BROOK MARIE BRIDGES'S CRISPY OVEN-FRIED CHICKEN DRUMSTICKS

Brook likes crispy chicken legs, but no pepper. And she likes this served with macaroni and cheese.

2   *tablespoons butter or margarine*
1/3   *cup cornflake crumbs*
1   *teaspoon paprika*
1/2   *teaspoon salt*
8   *chicken drumsticks*

■ Melt butter in the microwave. In a shallow bowl mix cornflake crumbs, paprika, and salt. Brush drumsticks with melted butter and then roll in crumb mixture. Place on a rack sprayed with vegetable oil. Bake at 450° for 25 minutes. Turn over. Bake for about 25 more minutes or until the interiors are fully cooked with no trace of pink.
Serves 4.

CUMIN EGGPLANT DIP WITH PITA TRIANGLES

Oven-roasting the eggplant and onion makes both delicious and mild. After peeling and cutting the roasted vegetables, all ingredients are pulsed in a food processor to a creamy chunkiness.

1   *package pita bread*
1   *eggplant (about 1¼ pound)*
1   *onion, peeled*
     Juice of 2 large lemons
1   *tablespoon olive oil*
1   *teaspoon ground cumin*
1   *teaspoon salt*
1/2   *teaspoon ground white pepper*

■ Stack half of pitas. Cut into 6 triangles. Repeat with remaining pitas. Prick eggplant with fork. Roast eggplant and onion in 350° oven until very soft, 35 to 40 minutes. Peel and cut into chunks. Place vegetable chunks, lemon juice, oil, cumin, salt, and pepper in food processor. Pulse until small chunks remain in the dip.
Serves 4 to 6.

STEAMED NEW POTATOES WITH DILL MUSTARD DIPPING SAUCE

Try to find the baby, bite-sized potatoes that have just emerged from the dark earth. These natural little packages are the perfect base for the honey-mustard dip.

2	*pounds small new potatoes, scrubbed*
⅔	*cup Dijon mustard*
2	*tablespoons honey*
1	*tablespoon freshly chopped dill*
½	*teaspoon pepper*

■ If the potatoes are somewhat large, cut each into 2 bite-sized pieces. Steam the new potatoes until they are tender, about 8 minutes. Let potatoes air-dry in steamer basket. Combine mustard, honey, dill, and pepper. Place potatoes in a dish with sides, such as a quiche dish. Serve sauce in a small bowl.

Note: For a fancy presentation, use a small red cabbage to hold the dip. Cut off a flat slice on the bottom, forming a balanced base. Slice off the top third of the cabbage. Remove enough of the center portion to hold the dip. Garnish the platter with sprigs of fresh dill.
Serves 12.

Longtime friends John Abbott and Katherine Chancellor share a quiet moment at her holiday party. When they were teenagers they dated briefly.

SAUSAGE TORTELLINI WITH WARM ITALIAN DIPPING SAUCE

Use the fresh tortellini available in the supermarket's refrigerated cases to create this fast starter. While bringing the water to a boil, pop the remaining ingredients into the microwave to produce an herbed sauce. Now there is plenty of time for sharing the news of the day.

1	*pound fresh, sausage-filled tortellini*
1	*14-ounce can crushed tomatoes in puree*
2	*tablespoons red wine vinegar or balsamic vinegar*
1	*tablespoon sugar*
1	*teaspoon dried Italian herbs, crushed*
1	*teaspoon salt*
½	*teaspoon dried red pepper flakes*

■ Follow package directions, cooking tortellini until al dente. Drain well. In a microwaveable bowl mix tomatoes, vinegar, sugar, Italian herbs, salt, and pepper flakes. Microwave on high for 4 minutes, stopping midway to stir. Place sauce in a bowl in the center of a large platter surrounded by tortellini speared with cocktail picks. *Serves 6.*

FRESH CORN GRIDDLE CAKES WITH AVOCADO CREAM

Use just-picked ears of corn to make these cakes. After shucking the fresh ears, break or cut each into 2 pieces. Place the flat surface on the cutting board to make a stable base for cutting off the kernels with a large, sturdy knife.

CAKES

6	*ears fresh sweet corn, shucked*
4	*egg whites, whipped until stiff, not dry*
½	*teaspoon salt*
½	*teaspoon pepper*

AVOCADO CREAM

1	*avocado, peeled and pitted*
1	*tablespoon lemon juice*
1	*teaspoon fresh marjoram or chervil*
½	*teaspoon salt*

■ Cut corn from ears. Gently fold into egg whites with salt and pepper. Drop by a tablespoon on a medium-hot, greased griddle. Cook for 2 minutes until golden brown on each side. Keep warm. Mash avocado with lemon juice, marjoram or chervil, and salt. Place a teaspoonful of avocado cream on each cake. *Serves 12.*

FETA CHEESE AND BABY SHRIMP PHYLLO TRIANGLES

The paper-thin phyllo dough requires careful handling. Thaw the frozen dough completely before beginning. Work with a single sheet at a time on a dry, clean work surface. Traditionally, butter was used to separate the layers, but here an easier technique is suggested—spraying with vegetable oil. Those preferring the taste of butter might opt to use all butter or a mixture of butter and oil.

4	ounces feta cheese, crumbled (about 1 cup)
6	ounces shrimp, cooked, chopped (about 1 cup)
1	teaspoon dried fine herbs de Provence, crushed
5	14x18-inch sheets phyllo pastry (3 ounces)
	Vegetable oil spray
2	tablespoons melted butter

■ In a medium bowl mix together the feta, shrimp, and herbs. Place 1 phyllo sheet on the cutting board. Cover remaining dough with dishcloth or plastic wrap to keep from drying out. Spray sheet with vegetable oil. Cut crosswise into 6 strips. Place a heaping teaspoon of feta and shrimp filling 1 inch from the beginning of each strip. Fold diagonally into triangles similar to folding a flag. Place on an ungreased baking sheet with the loose end tucked underneath. Brush tops with melted butter. Bake at 375° for 12 minutes or until browned.

Note: ½ cup of melted butter can be used in place of the spray. For smaller triangles, cut each strip into 8 pieces and use about 1 teaspoon of filling per appetizer.

Makes about 30 medium-sized pieces.

Diane was Jack's date at Katherine Chancellor's lavish New Year's Eve party in 1996.

ROASTED OYSTERS ON THE HALF SHELL WITH WHITE WORCESTERSHIRE DIP

Use sturdy work gloves and a strong oyster knife for shucking. After inserting the knife, wiggle it and twist off the oyster's rounded top. Save the bottom shells as the base for roasting and presentation. While oven roasting the oysters, a quick sauce is organized on the stove top. The white Worcestershire, remarkably different from its dark cousin, perfectly finishes the sauce.

2   *dozen fresh oysters, scrubbed*
    Rock salt
2   *teaspoons butter*
1   *shallot*
½   *cup white wine*
1   *teaspoon white Worcestershire*
    Pinch ground white pepper

■ Wearing heavy gloves shuck the oysters, cutting the muscle from the shell. Discard top oyster shell. On a large ovenproof platter, scatter a layer of rock salt. Nestle the larger part of each shell in the salt. Fill each shell with an oyster. Roast at 450° for 5 minutes or until the oysters are plump. In a small saucepan heat butter. Sauté the shallots for 1 minute. Add wine, white Worcestershire, and a pinch of white pepper. Place sauce in separate serving dishes and present with the oysters.
Serves 4.

FRESH MOZZARELLA, AVOCADO, AND TOASTED SUNFLOWER SEEDS WITH LIME-CILANTRO SAUCE AND SOURDOUGH TOASTS

The fresh taste of mozzarella and the creamy mouth feel of avocado is heightened with the zing of fresh lime and cilantro and the crunch of sunflower seeds and sourdough toast points.

½   *pound fresh mozzarella cheese,*
    sliced, room temperature
1   *large, ripe avocado, peeled,*
    pitted, and sliced
3   *tablespoons hulled sunflower*
    seeds, toasted
3   *tablespoons chopped fresh cilantro*
    Juice of 2 limes
½   *teaspoon salt*
½   *teaspoon ground black pepper*
8   *crisp triangles of sourdough toast points*

■ On 4 serving plates alternate and fan slices of mozzarella and avocado. Sprinkle with sunflower seeds. Mix cilantro, lime juice, salt, and pepper and drizzle over the fanned slices. Place 2 toast points on each plate. Serve immediately.
Serves 4.

JULY FOURTH AT THE NEWMAN RANCH

Like most Independence Days in Genoa City, the air was thick with tension and sparks were flying when Nikki hosted the Fourth of July celebration in 1997 at the Newman ranch. Nick begrudgingly invited Sharon's friend Grace to attend the barbecue, even though he was extremely uncomfortable around her. He feared that if he did not invite her, Sharon would ask questions that could lead to awkward revelations. Grace came with her former boyfriend Tony and six-year-old Cassie, whom Sharon didn't realize was the daughter she had given up for adoption years earlier.

The greatest shock at the party, however, was Victor's arriving with Diane. Victoria was particularly unsettled by Diane's being there, as was Jack Abbott, who made a hasty exit.

At Diane's office after the party, Victor tried to ease her jitters over the family's chilly reception of her by explaining that his children were simply curious about their potential new stepmother. This was the first Diane had heard of marriage, but the smile that filled her face suggested such a proposal was acceptable to her.

Menu

BEER AND BARBECUED BABY BACK RIBS

KRISTOFF ST. JOHN'S RED CHICKEN

KATE LINDER'S MEXICAN FIESTA DIP

GRILLED LEMON ROSEMARY MARINATED
CHICKEN BREASTS WITH FRESH ASPARAGUS

HEARTY RANCH-STYLE BEANS

CABBAGE AND GREEN-GRAPE SLAW

SLICED HOMEGROWN TOMATOES DRIZZLED WITH
BALSAMIC VINEGAR

ROASTED CORN ON THE COB WITH MELTED SWEET BUTTER

RED-RIPE SEEDLESS WATERMELON WEDGES

FRESH BLUEBERRIES WITH CREAM

RED, WHITE, AND BLUE JELLY BEAN COOKIES

LEMONADE OR BEER

Victoria and Cole greeted Katherine at the Newman's July Fourth party in 1996.

BEER AND BARBECUED BABY BACK RIBS

The pork ribs are first pampered in a steam bath of beer, where they leave unwanted fat in the process of becoming tender.

Meanwhile, a spicy sauce is created—a vinegary, tomatoey, and sweet brushable concoction with a hint of cinnamon. Slather this on the ribs, and subject the meat to elevation by fire. Often Cole Howard is spotted taking over some of the grill duties. Adding hickory, applewood, or mesquite wood chips for even more flavor is encouraged. The result is a messy finger-food affair—definitely not for those dressed in tennis or polo whites. Too bad.

2	racks baby back pork ribs (1½ to 1¾ pounds per rack)
2	cans Wisconsin beer
2	cups water
1	8-ounce can tomato sauce
⅓	cup cider vinegar
¼	cup brown sugar
2	tablespoons peanut oil
1	tablespoon prepared mustard
1	teaspoon chili powder
1	teaspoon salt
¼	teaspoon black pepper
½	teaspoon cinnamon
1	teaspoon (or more) Tabasco hot sauce

■ Place ribs in a turkey roaster or other large pan. Add beer and water. Bring to a boil. Simmer for 30 minutes until ribs are tender.

Jack and Ashley made a quick departure after Victor surprised everyone by bringing Diane as his date to the Fourth of July party in 1997 at the Newman ranch.

Remove ribs from beer bath. Discard beer bath. In a saucepan mix remaining ingredients for basting sauce. Cook over medium heat, stirring occasionally, until thickened, about 10 minutes. When coals or grill is hot, brush ribs with sauce and grill about 6 inches from the source for 15 minutes on each side. Baste occasionally with sauce, being careful to avoid burning the ribs. *Serves 6.*

KRISTOFF ST. JOHN'S RED CHICKEN

Kristoff St. John's son, Julian, named this baked chicken with barbecue sauce. Since the age of 2 he has said, "Give me the red chicken dish." Kristoff said "We usually have it with brown rice and broccoli, which my son adores, and salad. It's a general meal in our house."

3   pounds cut-up chicken pieces
    Salt and pepper
    Onion salt, optional (but not for kids)
1   cup barbecue sauce

■ Arrange chicken pieces on a rack sprayed with vegetable oil in a baking pan. Sprinkle with salt and pepper and optional onion salt. Bake at 375° for about 45 minutes. Using a pastry brush or spoon, cover with barbecue sauce. Bake 10 more minutes or until the center of the chicken is no longer pink.
Serves 4.

KATE LINDER'S MEXICAN FIESTA DIP

"This is an amazingly simple dish to prepare that looks great and also looks like you spent a lot of time in the kitchen," says Kate Linder. "It's perfect at home or to take to parties. No matter how much I make, it's always gone instantly."

1   medium to large can refried beans
3   avocados
2   teaspoons lemon juice
      Salt and pepper to taste
1   large container sour cream
1   package taco mix
1   bunch green onions
2   large tomatoes
1 to 2 cans sliced black olives
6   ounces of grated cheddar cheese
      for garnish
1   package tortilla chips

■ Take a large oblong or round platter and spread out a layer of refried beans on the bottom. Combine the avocados, lemon juice, salt, and pepper and spread the mixture on top of the beans. Combine the sour cream and taco mix. Spread that mixture on top of the avocado mixture. Chop and combine the green onions, tomatoes, and olives. Spread that mixture in a ring around the outside of the platter. Garnish the top with cheddar cheese and serve with tortilla chips.
Serves 6 to 8.

GRILLED LEMON-ROSEMARY MARINATED CHICKEN BREASTS WITH FRESH ASPARAGUS

This dish reminds Hope of the Kansas farm where, in the spring, she wandered out to the gardens to harvest tender asparagus and fresh rosemary.

4   chicken breasts, skinless, boneless
3   tablespoons lemon juice
1   tablespoon Dijon mustard
1   shallot, minced
1   tablespoon minced fresh rosemary
    (or 1 teaspoon dried)
½   teaspoon salt

1   pound fresh asparagus
1   lemon, cut into large wedges for garnish
4   sprigs rosemary for garnish

■ Between pieces of plastic wrap, pound chicken to a uniform ½-inch thickness. Marinate chicken in lemon juice, mustard, shallot, and rosemary in a plastic bag refrigerated for at least 1 hour. Grill about 8 minutes per side or until all pinkness is gone when the meat is sliced. Remove tough ends of asparagus. Steam about 10 minutes or until al dente. Divide asparagus onto 4 plates. Cut each breast into long strips and fan over asparagus. Garnish each plate with a lemon wedge and rosemary sprigs.

Note: Fresh lemon thyme makes a delightful herb variation.
Serves 4.

The Newman Independence Day party has become a tradition in Genoa City. In 1997 Grace (right) was an invited guest of Nick and Sharon's (left). The previous year Dru and Neil (far right) enjoyed spending the holiday at the Newman ranch.

CABBAGE AND GREEN-GRAPE SLAW

The Newmans make up a huge batch of this slaw for barbecues on the ranch. The dressing is made with nonfat sour cream and nonfat mayonnaise.

½	large head green cabbage, shredded (about 6 cups)
3	carrots, shredded
½	cup sliced green grapes
3	scallions, sliced
⅓	cup nonfat sour cream
⅓	cup mayonnaise
2	tablespoons sugar
2	tablespoons vinegar
1	tablespoon Dijon mustard
1	teaspoon salt

■ In a large bowl combine cabbage, carrots, grapes, and scallions. In a small mixing bowl whisk together sour cream, mayonnaise, sugar, vinegar, mustard, and salt. Pour over cabbage mixture and toss. Refrigerate about 2 hours before serving. *Serves 12.*

RED, WHITE, AND BLUE JELLY BEAN COOKIES

The powerful flavor punches of these gourmet jelly beans create a memorable cookie for the birthday of the nation—a nation that encourages entrepreneurs like Victor to emerge, conquer, and control. The cookie is buttery, rich, and crisp while the jelly beans are bursting with flavor and a chewy texture.

½	cup butter
⅓	cup sugar
1	egg
1	teaspoon vanilla extract
¾	cup flour
¼	teaspoon salt
¼	cup blueberry jelly beans
¼	cup cherry jelly beans
¼	cup white jelly beans

■ In a food processor or with an electric mixer, incorporate butter and sugar. Mix in egg and vanilla. Mix in flour and salt. Drop a heaping teaspoon on a greased baking sheet, permitting enough space for the cookie to spread to about 3½ inches. Press about 3 jelly beans into each cookie. Bake at 350° for 8 to 10 minutes or until the edges just begin to brown. Let cool on a baking rack. Store in a cookie monster–proof container. *Makes about 3 dozen.*

CHRISTMAS AT THE ABBOTTS'

*F*or a while it looked as if Christmas 1996 at the Abbotts was not going to be very special for anyone, even though the Abbott home during the holidays has traditionally been a wonderful place for the family. The spirit of Christmas usually fills the house. This year, however, Traci was spending the holiday out of town with her husband, Steve, and her daughter, Colleen. Meanwhile, John's former wife, Jill, made plans to enjoy a special trip with John Silva, but at the last minute she realized she couldn't be apart from her son, Billy. Ashley surprised her brother, Jack, with a generous gesture to demonstrate her support by inviting Diane to join the family on Christmas Day. John also invited his longtime friend Katherine Chancellor, who arrived bearing gifts. The mistletoe tradition was exploited by Jack and Diane, and John and Jill did their best to see that Billy enjoyed the holiday. The highlight of the celebration was John's special Christmas toast, offering his best wishes for family and friends.

Menu

Fresh Asian Pear and Green-Grape Compotes	String Bean and Mushroom Casserole
Cranberry-Apple Chutney	Butter and Maple Syrup Sweet Potatoes
Roasted Fresh Turkey and Port Gravy	Rolls and Creamy Wisconsin Butter
Sausage and Onion Dressing	Walnut Pumpkin Pie with a Snappy Ginger Crust
Honey-Glazed Ham	Sun-dried Cranberry-Cherry Bourbon Cake

At the Abbotts' Christmas celebration in 1996, Jack was deeply touched that his sister, Ashley, set aside her negative feelings toward his girlfriend Diane and included her in the family's festivities.

FRESH ASIAN PEAR AND GREEN-GRAPE COMPOTE

The adult version of this compote uses an inexpensive Spanish champagne while the young folks have theirs in orange juice. And to make sure that no slipups occur, the adult compotes are served in the cherished, Baccarat crystal "Marie Antoinette" champagne glasses, the coupes so named after her generous breasts. The orange versions are served in navel-orange half-shells placed inside an inexpensive small glass bowl.

1   *pound green grapes, cleaned and drained*
5   *large, crisp Asian pears, sliced paper-thin*
3   *tablespoons Spanish champagne per adult serving*
2   *tablespoons orange juice per child's version*
   Mint sprigs for garnish

■ Divide grapes and pear slices among champagne glasses for the adults and orange shells for the children. Add appropriate liquid. Garnish with mint.

   Note: If time and space permit, all glassware can be prechilled for a festive look.
Serves 8 to 10.

From the happy looks on Victoria's and Cole's faces at holiday time it's difficult to believe this beautiful couple could have any problems in their marriage.

CRANBERRY-APPLE CHUTNEY

So much controversy started to surround the question "which is the best sauce for the holidays, jelled or whole berry?" it became apparent that something new would be the only answer. Not only does this intriguing sauce close the controversy, it has became everyone's standard choice. The effort of preparation is minimal. After washing the berries and coring and chunking the apples, all that is needed is stovetop cooking, less than 30 minutes. Try it also as a sandwich sauce with thick slices of turkey or chicken meat.

  1   *pound fresh cranberries, washed*
  2   *apples, cored and chopped*
  1   *cup apple cider vinegar*
  ¾   *cup sugar*
  ½   *cup raisins*
  ½   *teaspoon cinnamon*
  ¼   *teaspoon ground cloves*
  ⅛   *teaspoon cayenne pepper*

■ Remove any damaged berries. Place in a large saucepan with all remaining ingredients. Stir. Bring to a boil. Simmer until the berries pop, the apples become tender, and the sauce begins to thicken, about 25 minutes. Let cool. Transfer to glass jars. Refrigerate.

Note: Tuck an extra bag of fresh cranberries in the freezer to make this superb sauce when the fruit is out of season.

Makes about 3 cups.

PORT GRAVY

The chefs like this gravy since it can be started as soon as the turkey is put in the roasting pan. First a simple stock is made from the turkey neck with aromatic vegetables, roughly chopped. A butter and flour roux is used to thicken the gravy—no need to use drippings from the turkey.

  1   *turkey neck*
  4   *cups water*
  2   *cups port*
  1   *small onion, chopped*
  1   *small carrot, chopped*
  1   *small celery, chopped*
  1   *bay leaf*
  ½   *cup butter*
  ½   *cup flour*
       Salt and ground white pepper, to taste

■ In a 3-quart pot bring turkey neck, water, port, vegetables, and bay leaf to a boil. Reduce heat and simmer for 45 to 60 minutes. Strain stock. Melt butter in pot. Slowly stir in flour. Continue to cook over low heat, stirring constantly for 5 minutes being careful not to burn the roux. Whisk hot roux into the hot stock. Continue until smooth. Adjust the salt and pepper. Add additional water if gravy is too thick.

Note: Putting the stock and roux in a blender or food processor is a foolproof method of having no lumps.

Makes about 5 cups.

SAUSAGE AND ONION DRESSING

This is a dressing that appeals to almost everyone in the family. Young and old like the reinforced taste of spicy turkey sausage along with the turkey gravy. The dressing is always baked separately since the old-fashioned method of placing stuffing in the turkey led to health problems—the internal temperature is insufficient to kill harmful bacteria.

1	pound bulk-ground Turkey Sausage (see page 42)
1	onion, diced
2	teaspoons salt
1	teaspoon ground black pepper
1	teaspoon ground sage
½	teaspoon ground thyme
½	teaspoon ground oregano
8	cups good-quality bread, cubed and oven-toasted at 350° for 10 minutes

■ In a large skillet sauté turkey sausage and onion until the meat is no longer pink. Drain off excess fat. Stir in seasonings and herbs. Mix with toasted bread. Spray a 9x12x2-inch dish with vegetable oil spray. Bake at 350° for 20 to 25 minutes until browned.
Serves 8 to 10.

STRING BEAN AND MUSHROOM CASSEROLE

Sure this is a 1950s retro food, but it's still a favorite with millions. Mary Williams often includes this among her potluck church dishes. It has been updated to use better ingredients. The canned string beans are replaced with the less metallic tasting frozen French-cut ones. Oh well, there is still cream of mushroom soup in it—the new

Hope and her friend Betty enjoy the holiday and watch as Victor presents his son, Victor Jr., with a Christmas gift.

low-fat one. And as long as we have gone this far, we opened a can of crispy fried onion rings and spread them on top. We still adore some foods.

2   10-ounce packages French-cut
    string beans, defrosted
1   can low-fat cream of mushroom soup
1   can fried onion rings

■ Spray a casserole dish with vegetable oil spray. Drain excess water from beans. Mix with mushroom soup in dish. Bake at 350° for 30 minutes or until hot and bubbly. Top with onion rings.
Serves 6 to 8.

BUTTER AND MAPLE SYRUP SWEET POTATOES

The finest ingredients, unencumbered with too many flavor notes, yield a supreme symphony of delight. Here is a side dish that always commands attention.

4   pounds of sweet potatoes,
    peeled, cut into ¼-inch slices
4   tablespoons salted butter, cut
    into small pieces
½   cup pure maple syrup
¼   teaspoon nutmeg

■ In a shallow casserole dish layer potato slices. Dot with butter. Pour syrup over potatoes. Sprinkle with nutmeg. Cover. Bake at 350° for 30 minutes. Uncover and bake for 20 minutes to form a glaze.
Serves 8 to 10.

WALNUT-GINGER PUMPKIN PIE WITH A SNAPPY GINGER CRUST

This is a gourmet pumpkin pie with a generous top layer of walnuts and a creamy pumpkin filling featuring one spice taste—ginger. The ground ginger is a flavor repetition of the gingersnap cookie crust. The crystallized ginger provides a candy ginger taste and texture.

CRUMB PIE SHELL
1   cup gingersnaps crumbs (about 20 cookies)
¼   cup butter, room temperature
2   tablespoons brown sugar

FILLING
1   15-ounce can pumpkin
1   12-ounce can evaporated milk
⅔   cup sugar
2   eggs
1   tablespoon blackstrap molasses
1   tablespoon chopped crystallized-
    ginger pieces
½   teaspoon ground ginger
½   teaspoon salt
2   cups walnut halves

■ In a food processor process gingersnaps until they are coarse crumbs. Add butter and sugar. Process until incorporated. Press mixture into the bottom of a 9-inch pie pan. Bake at 375° for 5 minutes. With an electric mixer combine pumpkin, milk, sugar, eggs, molasses, crystallized-ginger pieces, ground ginger, and salt. By hand stir in walnut halves. Pour into crumb shell. Bake at 375° until a knife inserted near the center comes out clean, 50 to 60 minutes.
Serves 8.

SUN-DRIED CRANBERRY-CHERRY BOURBON CAKE

This is a variation of the old bourbon cake that is served at the Kentucky Derby. It makes a tantalizing holiday fruitcake. Start drowning the fruit in bourbon 2 days before baking the cake. After creaming the butter with the sugar and eggs and incorporating the flour mixture, it might be helpful to move the entire affair to a giant mixing bowl or a turkey roaster. Using very clean hands, mix the batter with the fruit and nuts then fold in the egg whites.

1½ cups sun-dried cherries
1½ cups sun-dried cranberries
1   cup golden raisins
8   ounces bourbon
8   ounces butter
1¾ cups sugar
6   eggs, separated
2   cups flour
1   teaspoon baking powder
1   teaspoon salt
1   pound whole almonds

■ Soak dried fruit in bourbon for at least 2 days. With an electric mixer cream butter and sugar until light and fluffy, about 6 minutes. Gradually beat in egg yolks. Mix in flour, baking powder, salt, and the liquor drained from the fruit. Beat at a slow speed. With a sturdy spoon mix in fruit and almonds. Beat egg whites until stiff, not dry. Fold into batter. Line a 10-inch springform pan with parchment paper. Spray paper with vegetable oil. Spoon batter into pan. Bake at 300° for 2½ hours until a toothpick inserted in the center comes out clean. Let cool in the pan. Gently remove from pan. Wrap securely in plastic wrap until serving time. *Serves about 20.*

On the basis of the broad smile on Christine's face, it looks like she can't wait to open the large Christmas gift she's holding.

VICTOR'S SURPRISE BIRTHDAY PARTY

Hope planned to throw a surprise party for Victor's birthday until he announced that his former wife, Nikki, was planning a party for him at the ranch. She welcomed Hope's help with the food, and Nikki and her daughter took care of the decorations.

The guests included Hope, Nikki, Victoria, Cole, Sharon, and Katherine Chancellor. A bad cold prevented Douglas from attending. Hope made the first toast to Victor, and the honoree was deeply touched by the love and affection his family showed him. After the toast, Hope recieved troubling news that her close friend Cliff Wilson had been seriously injured in a tractor accident. When Victor saw how shaken she was, he immediately arranged to fly Hope to Cliff's bedside.

Menu

ASPARAGUS WITH FRESH MOZZARELLA, SUN-DRIED TOMATOES, AND FRESH BASIL

ROASTED-PEPPER AND SAGE-RUBBED FILET OF BEEF

POTATOES STUFFED WITH GARLIC-ROSEMARY
GOAT CHEESE

TENDER BUTTER LETTUCE SALAD WITH
BLUE CHEESE DRESSING

AWESOME FUDGE CAKE SNICKERED WITH
CHOCOLATE ICE CREAM

Nick and Sharon watch as Victor is playfully teased by Nikki at his surprise birthday party.

ASPARAGUS WITH FRESH MOZZARELLA, SUN-DRIED TOMATOES, AND FRESH BASIL

If asparagus spears have large stalks, peel with one of the easy-to-use, large-grip potato peelers. Be careful not to overcook so you retain the fresh, green, spring taste. Sun-dried tomatoes pack a powerful flavor punch. Use the olive oil in the chopped sun-dried tomatoes for the dressing.

> 1   *pound fresh asparagus*
> 4   *ounces fresh mozzarella, chunked*
> 2   *tablespoons chopped sun-dried*
>   *tomatoes with oil*
> 2   *tablespoons chopped fresh basil*

■ Steam asparagus for about 4 minutes. Stop cooking by placing in icy water. Drain. Arrange asparagus among 4 small plates. Sprinkle with mozzarella chunks, tomatoes in oil, and basil.
Serves 4.

ROASTED-PEPPER AND SAGE-RUBBED FILET OF BEEF

The filet is the finest cut of beef. It includes both the tenderloin and the filet mignon. Sold in the primal cut (commercial) form, it has too much fat and is enclosed by the tough silver skin. If possible, have the butcher prepare the filet by removing all the fat and silver skin. Remember to remove from the oven before an instant thermometer reaches the desired point since there will be some additional cooking while it stands.

> 1   *8-pound filet of beef*
> 3   *tablespoons coarsely ground*
>   *black pepper*
> 1   *tablespoon ground sage*
> 1   *tablespoon olive oil*
>   *Fresh sage leaves for garnish*

■ Place beef in a roasting pan. Rub with mixture of pepper, sage, and olive oil. Roast at 425° for about 45 minutes for medium rare. A meat thermometer will read 145° for medium rare. Remove from oven and let rest at room temperature for about 10 minutes, allowing the juices to be distributed throughout the meat. Slice on the diagonal. Garnish with sage leaves.
Serves 12.

POTATOES STUFFED WITH GARLIC-ROSEMARY GOAT CHEESE

Potatoes, always a favorite, can be dressed up for a fancy affair with cheeses and herbs. The trick to success is removing the interior of the potato while it is cooked, yet firm. This ensures a viable casing to hold the creamy filling.

4	*large baked potatoes, scrubbed*
⅔	*cup lowfat ricotta (or substitute cottage cheese)*
2	*ounces goat cheese*
1	*clove garlic, pressed*
1	*tablespoon chopped fresh rosemary*
½	*teaspoon salt*

■ Bake potatoes at 350° until just fork tender, 40 to 50 minutes. Cut each in half lengthwise, scooping out interior with a spoon. Leave a shell ½-inch thick next to the skin. In a small bowl mix potato with cheeses, garlic, rosemary, and salt. Stuff back into shells. Bake 10 to 15 more minutes until tops begin to brown.

Note: This recipe adapts quite successfully to the microwave. For a spectacular presentation, put cheese-potato mixture in a pastry bag fitted with a number 6 tube. Pipe back into the shell.
Serves 8.

TENDER BUTTER LETTUCE SALAD WITH BLUE CHEESE DRESSING

Nothing could possibly approach a better salad dressing than a rich, creamy blue cheese. This one is perfectly decadent and ideally suited for a special show-off party. Just imagine an entire pound of a pungent blue cheese!

1½	*cups sour cream*
	Juice of 2 lemons
1	*pound blue cheese, crumbled, divided*
1	*teaspoon black pepper*
6	*heads of butter lettuce, cleaned and spun dry*

■ In a food processor whip sour cream, lemon juice, half the blue cheese, and black pepper. Place whipped mixture in a small bowl. With a fork, mix in the remaining cheese. Cover and refrigerate for at least 1 hour to permit flavors to meld. Just before serving, place lettuce on chilled plates and mound with dressing.

Note: Low-fat sour cream can be substituted for a truly schizophrenic low-caloric dressing. Thin with several tablespoons of milk for a spectacular dip.
Serves 12.

AWESOME FUDGE CAKE SNICKERED WITH CHOCOLATE ICE CREAM

Birthday celebrations call for a magnificent cake-and-ice-cream creation that everyone can enjoy—particularly those avoiding cholesterol and excess fat. A meringue of egg whites and sugar is gently folded into the cocoa batter, which bakes into a light cake with enough body to withstand the tremendous weight of ice cream and candy. Assemble the cake a day ahead so the ice cream can harden.

3 *egg whites, room temperature*
1¼ *cups sugar*
2 *cups flour*
¼ *cup cocoa powder*
1 *teaspoon baking powder*
1 *teaspoon soda*
½ *teaspoon salt*
½ *cup vegetable oil*
1½ *cups milk*
½ *gallon low-fat chocolate ice cream, slightly softened*
2 *chilled, king-size Snickers bars (about 7.4 ounces each), finely chopped*

■ With an electric beater whip egg whites until stiff but not dry. Gradually whip in sugar. In another bowl combine flour, cocoa, baking powder, soda, and salt. Quickly stir in oil and milk. Gently fold in egg-white mixture. Pour into a greased 10-inch springform pan. Bake at 350° for 30 minutes or until a knife inserted into the center comes out clean. Let cool for 30 minutes. Remove from pan. Place on a cutting board. Cut horizontally in half with a large serrated bread knife. Cover the bottom of the springform pan with plastic or wax paper and reassemble bottom and sides. Put bottom cake layer in pan and spread with ½ of the softened ice cream. Sprinkle with ⅓ of the candy pieces. Place remaining cake layer on top. Spread with rest of ice cream. Press remaining candy into ice cream. Cover top of cake pan with plastic wrap and freeze for at least 4 hours. To serve, release the pan's spring and move cake to serving plate, holding the bottom piece of plastic wrap. Alternatively, the bottom part of the springform pan can be placed directly on the serving plate. Cut with a warm knife.

Note: Use the birthdayee's favorite candy as a topping. Also change ice cream flavors.
Serves 12.

Katherine Chancellor and Cole Howard were among the guests at the intimate birthday celebration for Victor that was jointly arranged by Nikki and Hope.

AN ELEGANT DINNER PARTY

*W*hen Victor Newman invited his friends and family to a surprise dinner party at The Colonnade Room's private dining room, they were instantly intrigued. Meanwhile, Jack Abbott, who worked closely with Victor, had not been invited, hinting that the purpose for the party was probably beyond just a friendly get-together. Nikki, Victor's former wife, was accompanied to the party by her husband, Dr. Joshua Landers, and made a dazzling entrance. The guests, however, continued to speculate about the reason for the event. When the party was in full swing, Diane arrived and realized the gala was meant to celebrate her marriage to Victor. When the host finally made the announcement, the room was very surprised.

Menu

BLACK SWEET CHERRY AND TOASTED ALMOND SOUP SWIRLED WITH COGNAC CREAM

BUTTER LEAF LETTUCE, ALFALFA SPROUTS, AND TOASTED ALMOND SLIVERS WITH FRESH CHERRY DRESSING

HERB-CRUSTED BEEF TENDERLOIN

GRILLED TILAPIA WITH A
BROWN SUGAR AND CITRUS SAUCE

WILD RICE WITH MOREL MUSHROOMS

DILLED ARTICHOKE HEARTS WITH BABY LIMA BEANS

PEACH AND RASPBERRY PIE WITH
FRAMBOISE CRÈME CHANTILLY

BLACK SWEET CHERRY AND TOASTED ALMOND SOUP SWIRLED WITH COGNAC CREAM

This rich fruit soup gives a festive, signature starter to The Colonnade's dinner parties. The portions suggested, given its soup-course status, are smaller than normal. The chef freezes extra cherries so the soup can also be served during the winter months.

3	cups pitted black sweet cherries (frozen cherries are fine)
1½	cups fresh orange juice, divided
¼	cup sugar
2	tablespoons cornstarch
½	teaspoon almond extract
½	cup sliced almonds, toasted
1	tablespoon cognac
1	tablespoon heavy cream

■ In a food processor puree cherries. In a 3-quart saucepan bring cherries, 1 cup orange juice, and sugar to a boil. Stir cornstarch into remaining ½ cup orange juice. Stir into soup and return to a boil. Cook 1 minute constantly stirring. Remove from heat and stir in almond extract. Divide into 6 bowls. Sprinkle with almonds and drizzle with cognac mixed with cream.
Serves 6 to 8.

BUTTER LEAF LETTUCE, ALFALFA SPROUTS, AND TOASTED ALMOND SLIVERS WITH FRESH CHERRY DRESSING

Needing to stay beautifully slim makes salad entrées uncommonly popular with the soap stars. This one is delightful during the summer months, when more of the local cherries are luscious, sweet, and abundant.

2	medium heads butter lettuce
½	cup cherries, pitted, divided
½	cup sour cream, reduced calorie
2	tablespoons white wine vinegar
1	teaspoon sugar, optional
½	teaspoon salt
½	teaspoon pepper
1	cup alfalfa sprouts
⅓	cup almonds, toasted

■ Break lettuce into bite-size pieces. Distribute among 6 salad plates. In a small food processor pulse half the cherries until almost a puree. Add sour cream, vinegar, sugar, salt, and pepper. Process until well mixed and smooth. Nap over salads. Cover with alfalfa sprouts and remaining fresh cherries. Sprinkle with almonds.
Serves 6.

GRILLED TILAPIA WITH A BROWN SUGAR AND CITRUS SAUCE

Farm-raised tilapia fillets have stormed the country. Tilapia is a sweet, delicate, white fish that grills in only minutes. Some food historians claim that this was the fish Jesus served to the multitudes on the Sea of Galilee.

2   *pounds tilapia fillets*
    Juice of 2 large lemons or 3 limes
3   *tablespoons brown sugar*
2   *tablespoons vegetable oil*
1   *tablespoon soy sauce*

Tony continues to have romantic feelings for Grace, although they are not reciprocated.

■ Make sure that all bones have been removed from the fillets. In a small mixing bowl combine lemon or lime juice, brown sugar, oil, and soy sauce. Dip each fillet in sauce. Grill 4 inches from hot coals about 2 minutes. Turn over and grill about 1 minute more.
Serves 6.

DILLED ARTICHOKE HEARTS WITH BABY LIMA BEANS

Here is an unusual combination that goes exceptionally well with a roast and bakes at the same time. In the winter all ingredients are from the freezer but still promise great textures and tastes.

1   *9-ounce package frozen artichoke hearts, defrosted, drained*
1   *10-ounce package frozen baby lima beans, defrosted, drained*
¼   *cup sour cream*
1   *teaspoon dill seeds*
1   *teaspoon salt*
½   *teaspoon black pepper*

■ Place artichokes and beans in a glass or ceramic baking dish. Mix sour cream, seeds, salt, and pepper. Pour over vegetables. Bake at 350° for 30 minutes or until the sauce is bubbling and the vegetables are hot.
Serves 6.

PEACH AND RASPBERRY TART WITH FRAMBOISE CRÈME CHANTILLY

Desserts from The Colonnade's pastry chef are elegant and sophisticated. Here the chef makes a French-style, buttery, cookie tart shell. It is filled with fresh peaches and raspberries mixed with sugar and lemon juice and baked into a magnificent, fragrant pie. Not willing to give guests less than the best, it is topped with crème chantilly, a freshly whipped, 36 percent butterfat-content cream lightly sweetened with Framboise, the delicate raspberry liqueur.

CRUST

1¼	cups flour
2	tablespoons sugar
6	tablespoons butter, room temperature
1	egg
1	tablespoon water, optional

FILLING

3	cups peaches, sliced
¾	cup raspberries (fresh or frozen)
¾	cup sugar
2	tablespoons flour
	Juice of 1 lemon

CRÈME CHANTILLY

1	cup heavy whipping cream
2	tablespoons confectioners sugar
1	tablespoon Framboise (or other raspberry liqueur)
	Fresh raspberries for garnish

■ Mix flour and sugar in a small mixing bowl. Cut in butter with a pastry cutter or fork until pieces are the size of large peas. Stir in egg. Add optional water if the dough is too dry.

Roll out on a lightly floured pastry board. Line a 10-inch tart pan or a 9-inch pie plate with dough. Bake at 400° for 10 minutes. In a medium-size bowl toss peaches and raspberries with sugar, flour, and lemon juice. Pour into tart shell. Bake at 400° until the filling starts to bubble, about 30 minutes. If crust begins to brown too much, cover edges with aluminum foil.

For crème chantilly, place cream in a chilled bowl and whip with chilled beaters until the cream is light and airy. Fold in sugar and Framboise. To serve, top warm slices of the tart with the crème chantilly. Garnish with a fresh raspberry.
Serves 8.

Nick and Sharon dance romantically at the lavish dinner party Victor held in honor of Diane, his new bride.

GREEN BAY PACKERS TAILGATE PARTY

Menu

GREEN-AND-GOLDEN SWEET PEPPER SALAD WITH
GORGONZOLA WALNUT VINAIGRETTE

"CHEESEHEADS" GREEN-AND-GOLD FOOTBALL

SMOKED BRATWURST WITH
GREEN-AND-GOLD CONDIMENTS

GREEN-AND-GOLD APPLE PIE
WITH CHEDDAR CRUST

*W*hen Malcolm was concerned over Olivia's tendency to avoid people after her husband's tragic death, he invited her to try something new, like learn to play pool—billiards. That evening, as he was offering his insights into the game, they met Robert Brooks, a player for the Green Bay Packers. Malcolm was a little starstruck, and Brooks was gracious, making fans of the couple immediately. Packermania had come to Genoa City! Since there is little chance of getting tickets to Green Bay's games, the people of Genoa City are inclined to cluster in front of their televisions whenever the Packers play. Of course, fans and football require snacks to complete the community Cheesehead experience, and many of them take advantage of the following recipes.

GREEN-AND-GOLDEN SWEET PEPPER SALAD WITH GORGONZOLA WALNUT VINAIGRETTE

This salad travels well and has just the right colors—especially for the Green Bay Packers' fans or those who simply have good taste. The peppers remain crisp in the vinaigrette while the walnuts add more texture and flavor.

2   green sweet peppers, seeded
2   gold sweet peppers, seeded
2   tablespoons walnut oil
1   tablespoon red wine vinegar
½   teaspoon black pepper
2   tablespoons Gorgonzola cheese
2   tablespoons chopped walnuts, toasted

■ Slice the sweet peppers. Mix together walnut oil, vinegar, and black pepper until smooth. Add cheese, leaving substantial lumps. Toss dressing with peppers. Sprinkle with walnuts. Chill. *Serves 6.*

"CHEESEHEADS" GREEN-AND-GOLD FOOTBALL

This football-shaped cheeseball might just set off a frenzy. Two of the state's star cheeses are mixed with the aid of a food processor with a secret punt of port.

1   *pound golden Wisconsin cheddar cheese, room temperature*
8   *ounces reduced-calorie cream cheese, room temperature*
1   *tablespoon port*
1   *cup toasted green pistachios*
2   *tablespoons black olive pieces*

■ Cut cheddar into large chunks. Place in food processor along with the cream cheese and port. Process until smooth. On a piece of wax paper or plastic film, shape cheese into a regulation-shape football. Roll in pistachios. Cut and press olive pieces to monogram the ball with the letter P. Refrigerate until time for kickoff.
Serves 8.

SMOKED BRATWURST WITH GREEN-AND-GOLD CONDIMENTS

6   *smoked bratwursts (about 1 pound)*
2   *fresh baguettes*
1   *squeeze-jar golden mustard*
1   *jar green pickle relish*

■ Grill bratwursts until well browned with crispy skin. Toast baguettes. Slice. Fill with meat, a squirt of mustard, and a dollop of green relish.
Serves 6.

GREEN-AND-GOLD APPLE PIE WITH CHEDDAR CRUST

For football fans, there is nothing more All-American than apple pie. The Packers' followers love the pie even more when the apple selection is green Granny Smiths and golden delicious.

Dough for double 10-inch piecrust
⅓   *cup grated sharp Cheddar cheese*
4   *cups Granny Smith apples, cored and sliced*
2   *cups golden delicious apples, cored and sliced*
⅔   *cup sugar*
1   *teaspoon cinnamon*
1   *tablespoon butter*

■ To the piecrust dough, quickly knead in cheddar cheese. Divide into half. Roll. Line 10-inch pie pan with crust. Fill with apples. Sprinkle with sugar and cinnamon. Dot with butter. Cover with top crust. Cut slits in the top crust to permit steam to exit. Bake at 425° for 10 minutes. Reduce heat to 350° and bake 45 to 55 more minutes until the interior is bubbly.
    Note: If apples lack natural sweetness, add up to ⅓ cup more sugar.
Makes 1 (9-inch) pie.

Romantic Meals

A meal in a romantic setting can work wonders for a relationship, especially if two people are feeling somewhat strained or if romance has somehow become elusive. Opportunities to mix food and feelings range from a simple picnic basket in the park to an elaborately planned evening with the finest Genoa City has to offer. A successful meal often concludes with passion rather than dessert, but moonlight and music are not the sole companions for romance, whether tender or tempting. Sometimes prying eyes spoil the affair, and promises made are not kept. These menus can help the moment happen for any couple, but there are no guarantees that the sparks will lead to fire.

CHRIS AND PAUL

Menu

HOT-SOUR SHIITAKI AND TOFU SOUP
·
COLD SPICY SINGAPORE NOODLES WITH
PORK AND PEANUTS
·
TANGERINE BEEF SIRLOIN WITH BROCCOLI AND
MUSHROOMS IN HOISIN SAUCE
·
STEAMED RICE
·
BALLOONS OF CHAMBORD-SOAKED
NAVEL ORANGES
·
FORTUNE COOKIES

*W*henever their hectic schedules allow, Paul enjoys surprising Chris with getaway trips. When they were engaged, he arranged a weekend trip to Minnesota, where they enjoyed the ballet. On a trip to Vietnam, where they found Luan's son, Keemo, Paul also took steps for them to enjoy a few restful and romantic days in Hawaii. These special moments keep the romance in their relationship, but they also provide a much-needed break from their demanding careers. This is healthy because Paul, a private detective, and Chris, a legal aid attorney, are both dedicated to their work and bend over backward to protect their clients' interests, which sometimes causes them to neglect their own relationship. Paul is not the only one sensitive to their needs. Chris has also surprised him at his office with a picnic basket and an invitation to take an hour away from work to enjoy lunch together at a nearby park.

HOT-SOUR SHIITAKI AND TOFU SOUP

There is nothing quite like a hot and sour soup to revive one's passions for life, particularly after a shocking event or just a cold day. Add cooked chicken or pork if desired.

½ ounce dried shiitaki mushrooms
1 quart chicken stock
1 10-ounce package firm tofu, cubed
3 tablespoons apple cider vinegar
2 tablespoons soy sauce
1 tablespoon sugar
½ teaspoon black pepper
¼ teaspoon cayenne pepper, optional
1 tablespoon cornstarch
¼ cup water
1 egg
1 teaspoon oil
2 chopped green onions
3 tablespoons chopped, fresh cilantro

■ Soak mushrooms for 10 minutes in boiling water. Drain. Cut into thin strips, removing and discarding stems. In a large pot bring stock to a boil. Add mushrooms, tofu, vinegar, soy, sugar, pepper, and optional cayenne. Simmer for 5 minutes. Mix cornstarch in water until smooth. Pour into soup. Stir until the soup thickens and becomes clear, about 3 minutes. Beat egg with oil. Slowly pour into soup. Pull egg with a fork to form strands. Add onions and cilantro. Heat 2 more minutes. Do not boil. Serve hot.
Serves 6.

COLD SPICY SINGAPORE NOODLES WITH PORK AND PEANUTS

The Colonnade's chef loves to prepare these spicy noodles studded with tender pork and crispy peanuts. The dried noodles resemble a bird's nest. Drop the nests in boiling water and stir carefully to uncoil them, but take care not to break the noodles—the length of an Oriental's noodle is proportional to his or her good luck. Slurping noodles is a time-honored Oriental tradition, and the longer the noodle, the better the slurp.

½ pound Oriental egg noodles
3 tablespoons dark sesame oil
½ pound lean pork loin, diced
2 cloves garlic, pressed
½ cup peanuts
3 tablespoons peanut butter
1 to 2 tablespoons red pepper flakes
2 tablespoons hoisin sauce
3 tablespoons soy sauce
2 tablespoons rice vinegar
1 small cucumber, peeled and diced
1 tablespoon minced fresh ginger root
2 scallions, chopped

■ Cook and drain noodles according to package directions. In a large skillet heat oil. Sauté pork, garlic, and peanuts until pork is just cooked, about 5 minutes. In a large serving bowl combine peanut butter, red pepper flakes, hoisin sauce, soy sauce, and rice vinegar. Add pork mixture to the sauce and stir. Toss with noodles, cucumber, ginger root, and scallions. Refrigerate for several hours before serving.
   Note: Dried egg noodles are available in most Oriental supermarkets. Substitute the narrow width egg noodles.
Serves 4.

TANGERINE BEEF SIRLOIN WITH BROCCOLI AND MUSHROOMS IN HOISIN SAUCE

Blending the marinade directly in a zipable plastic bag and stir-frying makes this a quick meal. The garlic can be smashed inside the bag by rolling with a whole tangerine outside the bag. Then the meat is added along with the peeled tangerine sections. Zip the bag and smash the tangerines with your hands. Team with fragrant jasmine rice or Chinese rice noodles.

1   *pound beef sirloin steak,*
     visible fat removed
2   *cloves garlic, peeled*
2   *tangerines*
1   *tablespoon peanut oil*
½   *pound mushrooms, sliced*
1   *pound broccoli florets*
3   *tablespoons hoisin sauce*
     Tangerine sections for garnish

■ Cut beef into thin strips across the grain. Place garlic in a one gallon plastic bag. Hold the whole tangerine like a baseball and use it to smash ingredients in the bag. Then put the meat and the tangerine sections, which you have made from the whole tangerine, in the bag. Close bag. Smash fruit with fingers outside the bag. Add beef. Close bag. Refrigerate for at least 2 hours. In a large nonstick skillet or wok, heat oil. Remove beef from marinade. Quickly stir-fry beef. Remove from skillet. Stir-fry mushrooms and broccoli until crisp-cooked. Return beef to pan. Stir in hoisin sauce. Serve immediately.
Serves 4.

BALLOONS OF CHAMBORD-SOAKED NAVEL ORANGES

Sunshine and love in every little orange section joins with the passionate raspberry and its liqueur to make this satisfying dessert. Each finished balloon looks like a model for a still-life painting.

4   *large red-wine balloon glasses*
4   *large navel oranges, peeled*
4   *tablespoons Chambord*
     (raspberry liqueur)
     Fresh raspberries for garnish
     Fresh mint sprigs for garnish

■ Refrigerate glasses for at least 1 hour before serving. With a small sharp knife remove all the white pith from the oranges. With a chef's knife cut each orange into 4 horizontal slices. Cut each slice into 6 or 8 pieces. Place oranges in a glass bowl with Chambord. Gently toss. Refrigerate at least 1 hour. To serve divide oranges among glasses. Garnish with fresh raspberries and mint.
Serves 4.

DRUCILLA AND NEIL WINTERS

*P*assion has never been a problem for Neil and Dru. Unfortunately, Dru's strong-willed nature has often created problems for Neil, a conservative executive at Newman Enterprises. He was not keen on her accepting out-of-town modeling assignments because he believed they would interfere with raising their daughter, Lily, but Dru accepted the assignments anyway. Her dedication to her career caused them to separate briefly, but Neil's feelings for Dru never abated. When he realized how much she meant to him, he wanted to show his commitment to her by arranging an elaborate and intimate dinner. A chauffeur picked up Dru and escorted her to The Colonnade Room's private dining room where she found a beuatiful gown and jewelry waiting for her. Neil wore a tuxedo and had engaged a small group of musicians to complement the candlelit dinner. After their meal, the couple danced for the remainder of the evening. Dru promised Neil that she would give her family more attention, and they discussed having another child. The promises, however, did not last beyond the night.

Menu

SHRIMP MERLOT

CHAMPAGNE AND KIR ROYAL

BRANDIED LENTIL, FRESH ORANGE, AND TARRAGON SOUP

MOROCCAN LAMB, APRICOT, AND
ALMOND COUSCOUS

HARICOT VERTS WITH BROWNED BUTTERED PISTACHIOS

FRESH RASPBERRIES AND VANILLA YOGURT
CREAM PIE WITH CHOCOLATE COOKIE CRUST

SHRIMP MERLOT

Served in a crystal dishes, the pink shrimp in a pool of red merlot is a passionate starter. The purple basil garnish heightens these rich hues.

1	*pound jumbo shrimp, peeled*
1	*teaspoon butter*
1	*shallot, minced*
½	*cup merlot (or other dry, full bodied red wine)*
½	*teaspoon salt*
4	*fresh purple basil leaves*

■ Wash shrimp and devein. In a medium saucepan in butter, sauté shallot for 1 minute. Add merlot, salt, and shrimp. Cook over medium heat stirring until shrimp turns pink, about 3 minutes. Chill for at least 1 hour. Divide shrimp among 4 crystal dishes. Add about 1 tablespoon liquid to each dish. Garnish with purple basil leaves.
Serves 4.

BRANDIED LENTIL, FRESH ORANGE, AND TARRAGON SOUP

Here is a hearty soup to serve on a cold day. Lentils, unlike other dried pulses and beans, require no presoaking. Just open the package, clean, and add the enhancements.

1	*tablespoon olive oil*
1	*large onion, chopped*
3	*cups water*
2	*cups orange juice*
2	*cups lentils*
½	*pound carrots, chopped*
2	*teaspoons dried tarragon, crushed*
1	*teaspoon salt*
2	*tablespoons brandy*

■ In a soup pot measure oil. Cook onion for 3 minutes over medium heat. Add water, orange juice, lentils, carrots, and tarragon. Simmer for 50 to 60 minutes or until the lentils are softened and the soup begins to thicken. Add salt and brandy 1 minute before serving. Serve while hot.
Serves 8.

Jabot executive Neil Winters in a loving moment with his wife, Drucilla, a very successful model.

MOROCCAN LAMB, APRICOT, AND ALMOND COUSCOUS

The intrigue of the royal cities of Morocco pale in comparison to Genoa City. But this is a delightful entrée for those searching for ethnic variety. And there are several Moroccan food emporiums nearby in Chicago.

2	*pounds lean lamb cubes*
1	*tablespoon vegetable oil*
1	*onion, chopped*
2	*cloves garlic*
1	*cup white wine*
1	*cup dried apricot pieces*
1	*teaspoon ground turmeric*
½	*teaspoon ground cumin*
½	*teaspoon ground coriander*
½	*teaspoon ground cinnamon*
2¾	*cups water*
1½	*cups quick-cooking couscous*
1	*teaspoon salt*
½	*cup almonds*
	Lemon wedges for garnish

■ Brown lamb in oil in a large skillet. Add onion and garlic and sauté 2 more minutes. Add white wine, apricots, and spices. Simmer covered for 15 minutes. In a medium sauce pan bring water to a boil. Stir in couscous and salt. Turn off heat. Cover and let sit until all water is absorbed, 5 to 6 minutes. Fluff with a fork. Mound the couscous on the center of a serving platter. Cover with lamb and sauce. Sprinkle with almonds and garnish with lemon wedges.
Note: Couscous is semolina pasta that is steamed then dried.
Serves 6.

HARICOT VERTS WITH BROWNED BUTTERED PISTACHIOS

In early summer these tiny French green beans start to appear. Baby domestic string beans can be used while sweet and tender. While browning the butter, do not leave the room. There is a mere flash second between golden brown and burned.

1	*pound haricot verts (substitute baby green beans)*
2	*tablespoons butter*
3	*tablespoons pistachios*
½	*teaspoon salt*

■ Steam haricot verts over a small amount of water until just tender, about 4 minutes. In a small skillet melt butter. Add pistachios and stir. Cook over low heat just until the butter begins to brown. Coat haricot verts with pistachio butter. Serve while warm.
Serves 4 to 6.

FRESH RASPBERRIES AND VANILLA YOGURT CREAM PIE WITH CHOCOLATE COOKIE CRUST

This is a light pie filled with creamy yogurt on a crust made from store-bought chocolate cookies. Start the yogurt draining the night before. The crust takes about 3 minutes to assemble, process, and form. It is baked for 10 minutes, cooled, and filled with the sweetened, thick yogurt. Finally, fresh, fresh, luscious raspberries top the affair.

CRUST
20 chocolate wafer cookies (about 6 ounces)
¼ cup sugar
4 tablespoons butter

FILLING
16 ounces plain yogurt
½ cup confectioners' sugar
1 teaspoon vanilla extract
2 pints raspberries

■ Place cookies in a food processor with sugar and butter. Process to a coarse crumb. Press into a 9-inch pie pan. Bake at 350° for 10 minutes. Drain yogurt overnight in a coffee filter placed in the refrigerator. Stir in sugar and vanilla. Pour into shell. Arrange raspberries on top. Refrigerate at least 2 hours before serving.
Makes 1 (9-inch) pie.

Dr. Olivia Hastings poses with her new husband, Malcolm, while her sister, Dru, stands behind her husband, Neil, who's also Malcolm's brother.

JILL AND KEITH DENNISON

*T*hey met during a business acquisition between Dennison Industries and Newman Enterprises. Keith was immediately charmed by Jill's keen business sense and alluring personality. To ensure that the deal swung in favor of Newman Enterprises, Jill exploited their attraction, wearing an extremely seductive outfit and arranging an intimate dinner for Keith. Romance followed quickly, and Keith seriously considered marriage. He was so smitten by Jill that he introduced her to his daughters, Megan and Tricia, who were less than thrilled with Jill's take-charge personality. When Jill found it impossible to continue living in the same house with her former husband, John, where they shared joint custody of their son, Billy, she accepted Keith's invitation to share his home temporarily.

Eventually Keith learned that he was in love with a very complex woman who was capable of being extremely charming or deceitful, depending on the circumstance and what she stood to gain from the situation. When he learned that Jill was Phillip's grandmother, whose stepfather was involved with Keith's daughter Tricia, he was furious that Jill had not told him so at the beginning of their relationship. Since then Jill has worked hard to maintain their relationship.

Menu

CRAB, CREAMY CORN, AND GINGER SOUP

·

ALEX DONNELLEY'S LEMON-MUSTARD
ROASTED TURKEY BREAST

·

ROASTED ITALIAN TOMATOES AND FENNEL

·

STEAMED ASPARAGUS WITH LEMON-DILL BUTTER

·

PASSIONATE CHOCOLATE MOUSSE

CRAB, CREAMY CORN, AND GINGER SOUP

This soup is easy to prepare from ingredients found in many pantries. Jill Abbot in her rags days used canned albacore packed in water in place of the crab—and it was still delicious. Nowadays Jill uses only fresh, lump crabmeat imported from the Chesapeake Bay. For an unusual garnish serve with Ginger Croutons (page 18).

2   cups chicken stock
2   15-ounce cans cream-style corn
2   tablespoons finely chopped ginger root
½   teaspoon salt
½   teaspoon ground black pepper
6   ounces crab, fresh, frozen, or canned
2   tablespoons dry sherry
    Ginger croutons for garnish (page 18)

■ In a large pot bring stock, corn, ginger root, salt, and pepper to a boil. Reduce heat to a simmer and cook for 10 minutes. Add crab and sherry. Simmer until heated through, about 2 minutes. Remove from heat and serve. Garnish with ginger croutons.

Note: Fresh oysters can be substituted and poached right in the soup. The result is incredible.
Serves 6 to 8.

ALEX DONNELLEY'S LEMON-MUSTARD ROASTED TURKEY BREAST

1   turkey breast, bone in (about 3 pounds)
    Juice of 1 lemon
2   tablespoons mustard
1   tablespoon soy sauce
    Fresh snip of rosemary
1   can chicken broth

■ Marinate turkey in mixture of lemon, mustard, soy, and rosemary overnight. Spray a 9x12-inch pan with vegetable oil. Pour chicken broth into the pan. Place marinated turkey breast on top of broth. Bake at 350°, basting every 15 minutes. Turkey should be roasted for 20 minutes per pound until the interior is completely cooked and no longer pink.
Serves 10 to 12.

ROASTED ITALIAN TOMATOES AND FENNEL

Fennel, a bulbous vegetable with a hint of licorice, when teamed with Roma tomatoes makes quite a romantic side dish. Roasting at a high temperature concentrates the flavors, and the fennel pieces stay crisp.

3   **Roma tomatoes**
½   **pound fennel, thinly sliced**
1   **tablespoon olive oil**
    Fresh oregano sprigs for garnish

■ Place whole tomatoes and fennel slices in a ceramic casserole dish. Drizzle with olive oil. roast at 450° for 25 minutes. Garnish with oregano sprigs.
Serves 2.

Jill used her seductive charms on businessman Keith Dennison to help Jack Abbott close a potentially lucrative business deal for Newman Enterprises.

STEAMED ASPARAGUS WITH LEMON-DILL BUTTER

Try to find the pencil-thin, just-picked asparagus. Remove any tough ends and cook briefly. After melting the sweet butter, the additions of lemon, dill, and salt make a sensual sauce for the crisp, green spears.

½   *pound fresh asparagus*
2   *tablespoons butter*
1   *tablespoon lemon juice*
1   *teaspoon dill*
½   *teaspoon salt*

■ Steam asparagus over 1-inch of water for 3 or 4 minutes or until still crisp-tender. In a small skillet melt butter. Stir in lemon juice, dill, and salt. Place asparagus on a service plate. Cover with lemon butter.
Serves 2.

PASSIONATE CHOCOLATE MOUSSE

Mousse should be light and airy—the exact contrast to the beginning of a hopefully long and enduring romance. This version is sinfully rich, made with either semisweet chocolate chips or baking squares, then lightened with beaten egg whites. Serve in beautiful crystal glasses and garnish with a chocolate curl.

4   *ounces semisweet chocolate chips or baking squares*
4   *tablespoons sweet butter*
4   *egg yolks, beaten until pale yellow and thick*
4   *egg whites, beaten until stiff, not dry*
1   *tablespoon Cointreau liqueur*

■ Melt chocolate and butter over a double boiler. Remove from heat. Stir in egg yolks. Whisk in ¼ of the egg white mixture and the Cointreau. Using a large rubber spatula, gently fold in remaining egg whites. Spoon into glasses. Cover and chill several hours before serving.
Serves 4 to 6.

NICK AND SHARON

From the moment Nick Newman was introduced to Sharon Collins at the Crimson Lights Coffeehouse, he was captivated by her. As their relationship developed, a teenage Nick displayed a romantic side surprising to find in someone his age. At Christmas he purchased an expensive, stunning red coat for Sharon and sent it to her anonymously. Unfortunately, Matt Clark, Nick's rival, boasted that he had given her the coat and persuaded her to go out with him. Later that night he viciously attacked Sharon in his car, and during the attack, her coat was torn. A few weeks later Sharon realized that Nick was the one who had given her the coat. When he invited her to a romantic meal at an upscale restaurant on the outskirts of town, Nick asked that she wear the coat. Throughout the evening Nick was extremely attentive and impressed Sharon with his tenderness; however, she was tormented by flashbacks of her ordeal with Matt, which finally caused her to bring their date to an abrupt end. With time their love grew, and Nick and Sharon married. Although they now have a baby son, Nick and Sharon keep their romance alive with intimate evenings, cuddling before the fireplace.

Menu

MARGARITAS

SALSA FRESCA WITH BAKED CHIPS

RED SNAPPER HUACHINGO TORTILLA-STRIP SOUP

SANDRA NELSON'S CHOPPED CUCUMBER AND TOMATO SALAD

**SLICED RED TOMATOES, JICAMA, AVOCADO, AND BLACK OLIVES WITH
CILANTRO-LIME MAYONNAISE**

**DAVID SHAUGHNESSY'S SMOKED SALMON AND MUSHROOMS
IN A CREAMY WINE AND DILL SAUCE WITH ANGEL-HAIR PASTA**

TEQUILA-LIME TOFU CLOUD MOUSSE

SALSA FRESCA

The four components of a salsa are the base, the chilies, the herbs, and the acid. The traditional New Mexican fresh salsa has tomatoes as the base, jalapeños as the chilies, cilantro as the herb, and lime as the acid. But Chef Bill Weiland of the Santa Fe School of Cooking encourages creativity, expanding the base to include tomatillos, mangoes, papayas, squash, corn, or black beans. Any chilies will work including fresh, dried or smoked versions. For herbs options might be basil, oregano, or marjoram. And the acid might be lemon, orange, pineapple, or vinegar. To make a thicker salsa, the chef suggested pureeing about half of the mixture and adding it back to the chunky half.

4	*Roma tomatoes, seeded and diced*
3	*cloves garlic, minced*
1	*onion, chopped*
2	*limes, juiced*
2	*jalapeños, minced*
3	*tablespoons freshly chopped cilantro*
1	*teaspoon olive oil*
½	*teaspoon salt*
½	*teaspoon black pepper*

■ Mix tomatoes, garlic, onion, and lime juice in a bowl. Lightly smash with a potato masher. Add jalapeños, cilantro, olive oil, salt, and pepper. Puree half of the mixture. Stir pureed mixture into the chunky mixture. Refrigerate for several hours.

Note: Add a small amount of water if the mixture is too thick. Serve with baked tortilla chips or on top of meat or fish. For additional spicy heat, add up to a teaspoon of chili caribe.

Makes 1½ cups.

RED SNAPPER HUACHINGO TORTILLA-STRIP SOUP

Full of fresh red snapper in a spicy broth, this robust soup can also be served as an entrée. While the classic Mexican-style recipe places the tortilla strips in the soup as a thickener, this soup uses them on top for a crispy sensation. For variety, load the soup with shrimp, scallops, or fish.

6	*8-inch flour tortillas, cut into ½-inch strips*
1	*tablespoon vegetable oil*
1	*large onion, sliced*
4	*cups fish or chicken stock*
1	*14-ounce can diced tomatoes*
2	*teaspoons ground chili powder*
1	*teaspoon ground cumin*
1	*teaspoon salt*
1	*teaspoon black pepper*
½	*pound red snapper fillets, cut into chunks*
2	*limes*
1	*cup grated Monterey Jack cheese*

■ Place tortilla strips on a vegetable oil-sprayed baking sheet. Bake at 350° for 12 to 14 minutes or until the strips become crispy. Measure vegetable oil into a soup pot. Sauté onion for 2 minutes. Add stock, tomatoes, chili powder, cumin, salt, and pepper. Bring to a boil. Reduce heat then simmer for 10 minutes. Add snapper and cook for 3 more minutes. Squeeze in lime juice. Ladle into soup plates. Sprinkle on cheese. Top with tortilla strips. Serve hot.

Note: Cilantro lovers will be well rewarded by adding several tablespoons of freshly chopped cilantro along with the fish.

Serves 6 for starter or 4 for entrée.

SANDRA NELSON'S CHOPPED CUCUMBER AND TOMATO SALAD

Try to find red, ripe tomatoes that have never been refrigerated for a supreme-tasting salad. The only dressing added is a touch of balsamic vinegar and freshly ground black pepper since it is frequently served with a linguine dish redolent of olive oil, garlic, anchovies, capers, fresh herbs, and cheese (see page 29).

2   large cucumbers, peeled and chopped
2   large red-ripe tomatoes, chopped
1   tablespoon balsamic vinegar
    Freshly ground black pepper

■ Toss all ingredients in a serving dish and serve immediately.
Serves 4.

SLICED RED TOMATOES, JICAMA, AVOCADO, AND BLACK OLIVES WITH CILANTRO-LIME MAYONNAISE

Wait until the reddest, juiciest tomatoes come to the farmer's market, from your own yard, or from a fabulous neighbor before making this salad. For optimal flavor, never refrigerate the tomatoes.

12   *large lettuce leaves*
3   *large red-ripe tomatoes, thickly sliced*
1   *jicama, peeled and julienned*
2   *avocados, peeled, pitted, and sliced*
¼   *cup black olives, pitted*
½   *cup mayonnaise*
     (reduced-fat recommended)
4   *tablespoons lime juice (about 2 limes)*
½   *bunch fresh cilantro*
½   *teaspoon salt*
¼   *teaspoon cayenne pepper*
6   *sprigs cilantro for garnish*

■ Place 2 lettuce leaves on each salad plate. Fan tomatoes and jicama with avocado slices and olives on top. In a small blender or food processor pulse mayonnaise, lime juice, cilantro, salt, and pepper until smooth. Drizzle on each salad. Garnish with cilantro sprigs.

Note: The dressing may be painted on the salads using a squirt bottle, such as for ketchup.

More lime juice may be extracted by microwaving the limes for 15 seconds before squeezing.
Serves 6.

DAVID SHAUGHNESSY'S SMOKED SALMON AND MUSHROOMS IN A CREAMY WINE AND DILL SAUCE WITH ANGEL-HAIR PASTA

David says, "This is my own creation, so the amounts are rough, but they should work fine."

2	tablespoons butter
2	shallots, chopped
8	ounces fresh mushrooms, chopped
1	yellow pepper, chopped
	Cracked black pepper, to taste
1	8-ounce bottle clam juice
1	cup chardonnay
1	cup heavy cream
8	ounces smoked salmon, chopped
2	tablespoons chopped fresh dill
12	ounces angel-hair pasta, cooked al dente and drained
	Salmon caviar for garnish

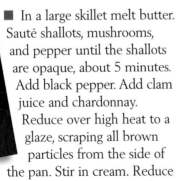

■ In a large skillet melt butter. Sauté shallots, mushrooms, and pepper until the shallots are opaque, about 5 minutes. Add black pepper. Add clam juice and chardonnay. Reduce over high heat to a glaze, scraping all brown particles from the side of the pan. Stir in cream. Reduce over medium heat until the mixture coats the back of a spoon. Stir in smoked salmon and fresh dill. Stir gently and heat through. Gently toss the salmon sauce with the pasta. Spoon onto plates and garnish with a teaspoon of caviar on top.
Serves 4 to 6.

TEQUILA-LIME TOFU CLOUD MOUSSE

See if anyone can guess the high-protein base of this dessert. For children omit the tequila and add 1 teaspoon vanilla extract.

1	cup frozen limeade concentrate, defrosted
1	pound soft tofu (blot to remove extra water)
3	tablespoons sugar
1	tablespoon tequila
	Fresh lime slices dipped in sugar for garnish

■ Process limeade, tofu, sugar, and tequila in a blender or food processor until smooth. Pour into dessert cups or glasses. Refrigerate several hours. Garnish with lime slices.
Serves 4.

VICTOR AND DIANE

From the beginning Victor and Diane's whirlwind romance has been charged with intrigue and an element of surprise. It began with a business lunch, where the conversation quickly turned flirtatious. Diane continued dining with Victor despite her being engaged to Jack Abbott. On one occasion, Victor arranged for her to join him on an impromptu trip to London aboard his private jet. It was a pivotal moment, and Diane was swept away by Victor's spontaneous gesture, but she tried to keep their involvement a secret from Jack. Nevertheless, Jack found Victor and Diane at a restaurant and confronted her. An argument erupted, and she ended their engagement. After Victor proposed to Diane and she accepted, he considered ending their romance when, from outside her office, he saw Jack and Diane in a kiss. He was able to set aside his jealous feelings and surprised Diane by inviting her to join him on the Newman jet for another trip, supposedly on business. By the end of the flight, however, they were married. Victor and Diane enjoyed a romantic honeymoon in Greece and then returned to Genoa City, stunning family and friends with the news of their nuptials.

Menu

WARM GOAT CHEESE ON WILTED SPINACH WITH CARAMELIZED ONIONS

FRESH GRILLED TUNA ON CURRIED CARROT AND SUNFLOWER-SEED PANCAKES WITH GARLIC-YOGURT SAUCE

CAULIFLOWER AND CRISPY BACON WITH SHALLOT AND WINE REDUCTION

LEMONY CUSTARD CAKE CLOUDS WITH MARINATED STRAWBERRIES

WARM GOAT CHEESE ON WILTED SPINACH WITH CARAMELIZED ONIONS

The cooking is all range-top in one skillet. And the results are elegant. Start by caramelizing the onions using only their natural sugars. Particularly good sweet onions are the Maui, Vidalia, Granex, Walla Walla, or Texas 10–15 varieties. The goat cheese, cut into rounds, is sautéed next. Finally the fresh spinach is wilted with the water clinging from its bath. A final toss in fruity, raspberry vinegar creates the perfect anchor for this taste sensation.

2	large sweet onions, peeled and thinly sliced
2	tablespoons olive oil
10	ounces goat cheese, sliced into 8 rounds
1	pound fresh baby spinach leaves, cleaned, still wet
2	tablespoons raspberry vinegar (or substitute red wine vinegar) Freshly ground black pepper

■ In a large, heavy skillet cook onions in olive oil over very low heat for 15 to 20 minutes or until the natural sugar starts to brown. Remove onions. Cook cheese rounds until lightly browned on one side, about 2 minutes. Remove from pan. Place spinach with clinging water in pan. Cover for 2 minutes or until wilted. Drain off any liquid. Stir in vinegar. Divide spinach onto 4 plates. Top each with 2 goat cheese rounds, browned side up, and caramelized onions. Grind black pepper over each.
Serves 4.

FRESH GRILLED TUNA ON CURRIED CARROT AND SUNFLOWER-SEED PANCAKES WITH GARLIC-YOGURT SAUCE

Everyone loves the sweetness of carrots with a hint of curry and crunchy sunflower seeds as the launchpad for the flavorful, rare tuna steaks. The light garlic-yogurt sauce ties it all together while adding a lemony tang. Caution is advised when making the cakes, which should be firm. Keep the vegetables in good-sized pieces and do not overcook.

4	tuna steaks (about 1⅓ pounds)
2	carrots, peeled, cut in large chunks
1	medium onion, peeled, cut in large chunks
1	egg
1	tablespoon oil
1	tablespoon flour
½	cup hulled sunflower seeds
2	teaspoons curry powder
½	teaspoon salt
½	cup nonfat plain yogurt
2	cloves garlic, pressed
2	teaspoons fresh lemon juice
2	scallions, minced for garnish

■ Grill tuna until medium rare inside. Place carrots and onion in food processor. Pulse/chop until they are the size of large peas. Mix in egg, oil, flour, seeds, curry powder, and salt until just incorporated. Cook on a medium-hot, oiled griddle using about ¼ cup batter for each cake. Flatten cake with the back of a large spatula. Cook until the batter sets and starts to brown on the exterior, about 4 minutes. Turn over. Cook until browned, about 3 minutes.

For sauce, mix yogurt, garlic, and lemon juice. To present, angle tuna on top of the carrot pancake. Drizzle with yogurt sauce. Garnish with scallions.
Serves 4.

CAULIFLOWER AND CRISPY BACON WITH SHALLOT AND WINE REDUCTION

Cauliflower is not boring when teamed with crispy bacon, mild shallots, and white wine. All the cooking, done on the range-top, takes less than 15 minutes including preparation time.

1   head cauliflower, trimmed
1   tablespoon olive oil
1   shallot, minced
¼   cup dry white wine
6   slices crispy bacon, broken into pieces

■ Separate cauliflower into florets. Steam in a 3-quart saucepan over 1 inch of water for 5 minutes or until al dente. In a small sauté pan heat oil. Sauté shallot for 2 minutes over high heat. Stir in wine. Cook for 3 minutes or until the mixture is reduced by half. Pour over cauliflower. Crumble bacon on top.
Serves 4.

LEMONY CUSTARD CAKE CLOUDS WITH MARINATED STRAWBERRIES

Romance keeps many minds aloft in the clouds. For this union we hope there will be only those sweet clouds. A cakelike batter is first assembled and baked either in a soufflé dish or individual ramekins. The result is a custardy base with a cakelike layer. Fresh, luscious strawberries spend at least one hour soaking up a dry white wine marinade for a spectacular topping.

CAKE
1   cup sugar
3   tablespoons butter
3   egg yolks
2   tablespoons flour
1   cup milk
    Juice of 3 large lemons
3   egg whites, beaten to a soft peak

TOPPING
1   pint strawberries, hulled and sliced
½   cup dry white wine
2   tablespoons sugar
zest of 1 lemon

■ In a large bowl cream sugar and butter. Beat in egg yolks one at a time. Stir in flour until incorporated. Stir in milk and lemon juice. Gently fold in egg whites. Bake at 350° in a 1½-quart soufflé dish in a bain-marie for 50 minutes, until the cake just begins to brown on the top. For topping, mix strawberries, white wine, sugar, and lemon zest. Let sit for at least 1 hour. To serve, spoon cooled custardy cake clouds into serving dishes and cover with marinated strawberries.
Serves 8.

Weddings and Honeymoons

Emotionally charged weddings and romantic honeymoons are the ultimate payoff for power-fully dramatic love stories. When a couple overcomes the tremendous obstacles that could adversely affect their love and finally makes a lifetime commitment, marriage marks the beginning of a joyful and exciting new chapter in their lives. Again the celebration of something so personal and intimate includes the culinary as well as the carnal, and complex menus are designed to enhance the occasion.

OLIVIA AND MALCOLM

Menu

CHILLED SHRIMP WITH FRESH MANGO SALSA

FRESH STRAWBERRIES, ROMAINE, AND WATERCRESS
WITH
MINT YOGURT DRESSING

SAUTÉED HERBED PORK LOIN WITH SHALLOT AND
GRAPEFRUIT BLACK BEANS

ALMOND WEDDING COOKIES

BRYANT JONES'S ICE CREAM COOKIE SANDWICHES

CAPPUCCINO ICE

WEDDING CAKE

CHAMPAGNE

Olivia and Malcolm were married in a small ceremony witnessed by family and friends. Olivia's son from an earlier marriage, Nate, served as ring-bearer, Malcolm's brother Neil was best man, Olivia's sister, Dru, was matron of honor, and Lily, Olivia's niece, was the flower girl. Malcolm and Olivia had only been romantically involved for a few months when they married, but their relationship was built on a strong friendship. Malcolm had been particularly supportive of Olivia following the death of her first husband, Nathan, who was fatally struck by a car. Olivia also appreciated the strong bond Malcolm had developed with Nate, who had difficulty accepting his dad's death.

CHILLED SHRIMP WITH FRESH MANGO SALSA

Mangoes are notoriously difficult to cut into beautiful presentation slices. So why bother? Here the mango is chunked then married with sweet, sour, salty, and spicy tastes with a bit more flavor from cucumbers and green onions. But the large, chilled shrimp still take center stage. And the larger the shrimp, the more impressive is this starter.

1	pound shrimp, cooked, peeled, deveined
1	large ripe mango, peeled, chunked
1	tablespoon sugar
	Juice of 1 lime
½	teaspoon salt
½	teaspoon black pepper
½	cucumber, peeled, seeded
1	jalapeño pepper, seeded, with ribs removed
1	green onion, minced

■ Chill shrimp. Place mango in a small bowl. Mix in sugar, lime juice, salt, and pepper until incorporated. Stir in cucumber, jalapeño, and green onion. Divide mango salsa among 6 chilled plates. Arrange shrimp on top. Refrigerate until serving time.
Serves 6.

FRESH STRAWBERRIES, ROMAINE, AND WATERCRESS WITH MINT YOGURT DRESSING

The peppery notes of watercress are mellowed by the strawberries' sweetness. And the whole affair is zinged with the tang of yogurt and the aromatic bite of mint.

1	head romaine lettuce
1	pint fresh strawberries, hulled and sliced
1	bunch watercress, torn into bite-size pieces
½	cup nonfat plain yogurt
3	tablespoons frozen orange juice concentrate, defrosted
2	tablespoons finely chopped fresh mint (peppermint, orange mint, spearmint)
1	tablespoon sugar
½	teaspoon salt
¼	teaspoon ground white pepper

■ Wash and dry lettuce. In a large bowl toss lettuce, strawberries, and watercress. In a small bowl mix yogurt, orange juice concentrate, mint, sugar, salt, and pepper. Pour over salad and toss.
Serves 6.

SAUTÉED HERBED PORK LOIN WITH SHALLOT AND GRAPEFRUIT BLACK BEANS

The flavor tastes of grapefruit and sweet shallots with black beans and pork intrigue the diners in Genoa City. It is not a complicated dish to prepare, and most of the effort can be done in advance.

1½	*pounds pork loin, trimmed*
2	*grapefruits, divided*
4	*shallots, chopped*
1	*tablespoon chopped fresh rosemary*
¼	*cup flour*
1	*teaspoon salt*
½	*teaspoon black pepper*
2	*tablespoons olive oil*
1	*can black beans, drained*
1	*teaspoon salt*
1	*teaspoon coarsely ground black pepper*
	Sprigs of fresh rosemary for garnish

■ Remove all fat from the meat and slice into 2-inch pieces on the diagonal. Marinate refrigerated for several hours with juice of one grapefruit, shallots, and rosemary. Remove meat from marinade. Reserve marinade. Pat meat dry with a paper towel. Dust with mixture of flour, salt, and pepper. Heat oil in a 10-inch frying pan. Sauté pork for about 2 minutes on each side or until the inside is just lightly pink. Remove pork and keep warm. Add reserved marinade, black beans, salt, and pepper to pan. Bring to a boil and scrape all flavor morsels from the pan. Reduce sauce by half. Add sections from remaining grapefruit and heat 2 minutes. To serve, divide hot bean mixture among four dinner plates. Arrange pork on top. Garnish with rosemary sprigs.

Note: If time permits, prepare black beans from their dried state.
Serves 4.

ALMOND WEDDING COOKIES

These delicate cookies make the anticipation of an upcoming wedding even more special. With butter at room temperature, the mixing is quite easy.

1	*cup butter, room temperature*
1	*cup confectioners' sugar*
1	*teaspoon almond extract*
2	*cups flour*
1	*cup slivered almonds*
¼	*cup confectioners' sugar for dusting*

■ With an electric mixer cream butter and sugar until light and fluffy. Beat in extract. Stir in flour and almonds until incorporated. Divide dough into thirds. Roll each into a log shape 20 inches x 1 inch. Cover with plastic wrap. Refrigerate for at least one hour. On a pastry board, cut each log vertically in half. Cut cookies into ½-inch pieces. Place flat side down on an ungreased baking sheet. Bake at 375° for 12 minutes or until just browned on the edges. Cool on a rack. Dust with confectioners' sugar.

Note: Toasting the almonds prior to mixing gives a richer taste to these cookies.
Makes 60.

BRYANT JONES'S ICE CREAM COOKIE SANDWICHES

Bryant likes a sweet taste, particularly ice cream, either chocolate or vanilla. Fill store-bought cookies with ice cream. Wrap individually and serve. Kids will enjoy licking around the edges as the ice cream melts. Younger ones love drips and messes, but that's what childhood is all about. Make a batch of these for snacks. For healthy snacks try the low-fat chocolate or vanilla wafers or graham crackers and fill with low-fat ice cream or yogurt.

- 2   *store-bought cookies such as chocolate chip or chocolate wafers*
- 2   *tablespoons ice cream, vanilla or chocolate, slightly softened*

■ Place one cookie on plate. Spread with ice cream. Cover with other cookie. Wrap in plastic wrap and freeze until needed.
Makes 1 cookie.

CAPPUCCINO ICE

This icy treat will satisfy any coffee lover. Brew with decaffeinated espresso beans for those fearing late-night jitters. Serve in a wine glass or dainty cappuccino cups.

2½   *cups strong coffee*
½   *cup sugar*
½   *cup milk*
¼   *teaspoon ground cinnamon*

■ Brew coffee and permit to cool. In a small pan over medium heat, dissolve sugar in milk. Stir in cinnamon. Stir in coffee. Cool. Pour into a small ice cream or sorbet maker and follow manufacturer's instructions.
Serves 6.

Malcolm poses with his sister-in-law, Drucilla Winters.

VICTORIA AND COLE

Menu

MINTED, CHILLED BABY GREEN PEA SOUP

TERIYAKI CALICO SCALLOPS IN MINI PASTRY SHELLS

LAURELEE BELL'S DIJON MUSTARD, GARLIC, AND
ROSEMARY ROASTED PORK

ROASTED CHICKEN WITH SWEET POTATO WEDGES,
FRESH PINEAPPLE, AND BANANA

TONYA LEE WILLIAMS'S GREEK SALAD

BAKED FRESH PEAR AND
ALMOND CUSTARDS

WEDDING CAKE

*V*ictoria and Cole actually had two wedding ceremonies. The first was a quick ceremony in Las Vegas, and the honeymoon was equally short-lived. Victoria's father, Victor, informed Cole that he had once been intimate with Cole's mother, Eve, and there was a possibility they might be father and son, which would make Cole Victoria's half-brother. Until the matter could be resolved with blood tests, the marriage was annulled. Victoria was shattered by the annulment and went into hiding. The tests, however, revealed that Cole wasn't Victor's son. Private detective Paul Williams was hired to find Victoria, and when his efforts gave them a general idea of where she might be, Victor hired a skywriter. Victoria saw the message and immediately contacted Cole. Soon after, she and Cole enjoyed a second ceremony in a small chapel, with Victoria's first husband, Ryan McNeil, and his wife, Nina, serving as witnesses. Victoria did not invite her parents to attend, but unknown to her, Victor quietly stood in the back of the church and witnessed the exchange of their vows.

MINTED, CHILLED BABY GREEN PEA SOUP

In the heat of the summer when appetites languish right along with the desire to cook, the Genoa City folks often opt for this country cousin to vichyssoise. The effort is minimal to produce this pale green, creamy soup. So give the maid the day off while still giving yourself a treat.

1   10-ounce package frozen baby green peas
2   cups nonfat plain yogurt
1   cup chicken stock
2   tablespoons chopped fresh mint
1   teaspoon salt
1   teaspoon pepper
    Peas for garnish
    Sprigs of fresh mint for garnish

■ Slightly thaw peas. Toss all ingredients into a food processor or blender and pulse until smooth. Serve chilled in clear glass cups or wine glasses. Garnish with a few peas and sprigs of fresh mint.
Serves 4.

TERIYAKI CALICO SCALLOPS IN MINI PASTRY SHELLS

Look for the prebaked mini pastry shells in the gourmet section of the supermarket. These are filled with the petite scallops on a nest of finely shredded lettuce.

1   pound calico scallops
    (small bay scallops)
1   tablespoon teriyaki sauce
2   leaves romaine lettuce
1   dozen mini pastry shells

■ In a nonstick skillet cook scallops in the teriyaki sauce until opaque, about 3 minutes. Remove scallops with a slotted spoon. Tightly roll lettuce leaves. Cut into narrow shreds. On a serving platter fill shells with a small nest of lettuce. Top with the scallop mixture.
Makes 12.

LAURALEE BELL'S DIJON MUSTARD, GARLIC, AND ROSEMARY ROASTED PORK

3   **pounds boneless pork roast**
½   **jar Dijon mustard**
5   **tablespoons crushed garlic**
2   **tablespoons chopped fresh rosemary**
1   **tablespoon soy sauce**

■ Trim all visible fat from the pork. In a small bowl mix Dijon mustard, garlic, rosemary, and soy sauce. Spray a large roasting pan with vegetable oil. Place roast in pan and coat with mustard mixture. Roast at 350° about 40 minutes—until a meat thermometer reaches 155° and the center is pink. *Serves 8.*

ROASTED CHICKEN WITH SWEET POTATO WEDGES, FRESH PINEAPPLE, AND BANANA

On a recent Caribbean trip, Ashley so enjoyed this roasted chicken with tropical fruits that she obtained the recipe from the chefs. After several attempts, here is exactly what she created at home.

1   **3-pound roasting chicken**
2   **large sweet potatoes, peeled**
1   **pineapple, peeled and cored,**
     cut into wedges
1   **small, underripe banana**
     Juice of 1 lemon

■ Clean chicken and pull out excess fat. Place chicken and potato wedges sprayed with vegetable spray on a rack in a roasting pan. Roast in a 375° oven for 1½ hours until the skin is crisp and the juices run clear. During the last 5 minutes, place pineapple and banana tossed with lemon juice in the oven until heated. Carve the chicken into serving pieces. Present on a large platter surrounded by potatoes and fruits. *Serves 4.*

TONYA LEE WLLIAM'S GREEK SALAD

Here is another excellent example of how she tears up hearts. There should be five or six cups of torn lettuce.

2   *hearts of romaine lettuce, washed and spun dry*
1   *red pepper, roasted, seeded, peeled, sliced into strips*
1   *cucumber, peeled, cut into chunks*
1   *large, red-ripe tomato, cut into chunks*
½   *cup black Kalamata olives, pitted*
¼   *cup extra virgin olive oil (use a fruity green one)*
2   *tablespoons fresh lemon juice*
1   *teaspoon chopped fresh oregano*
½   *teaspoon freshly ground black pepper*
4   *ounce block of feta cheese*

■ In a large salad bowl, break lettuce hearts into bite-sized pieces. Add pepper, cucumber, tomato, and olives. For dressing mix together olive oil, lemon juice, oregano, and black pepper. Pour dressing over salad. Toss until well coated. Crumble feta over salad. Serve.

Note: If in a hurry, use a 4-ounce jar of roasted red peppers. Drain well before adding to salad. An interesting variation is to use crumbled feta flavored with tomato and basil.

Serves 4 as side salad or 2 as an entrée.

BAKED FRESH PEAR AND ALMOND CUSTARDS

This is a classic custard dessert with a pear accent and an almond crunch. Using evaporated milk makes it richer than using whole milk. Low-fat evaporated milk works quite well. Try with any fresh, soft fruits including strawberries, raspberries, plums, or peaches.

3   *eggs*
1½ *cups evaporated milk*
⅓   *cup sugar*
1   *teaspoon vanilla extract*
2   *very ripe pears, peeled, cored, chopped*
2   *tablespoons sliced almonds*
   Dusting of ground nutmeg

■ Whisk together eggs, milk, sugar, and vanilla until completely blended. Divide pears into ovenproof, 6-ounce ramekins. Cover with egg mixture. Sprinkle with almonds and a dusting of nutmeg. Bake in a water bath at 350° for 35 to 45 minutes or until the custard is firm and a knife inserted near the center comes out clean.

Note: The custard mixture may also be combined in a food processor or blender. To make the water bath, place ramekins in a large baking or roasting pan with sides almost as tall as the ramekins. Fill with very hot water almost to the top of the ramekins.

Serves 6.

NINA AND RYAN

Menu

ROASTED OYSTERS ON THE HALF SHELL WITH WHITE
WORCHESTERSHIRE DIP (PAGE 58)

CRUDITES WITH DIPPING SAUCE

FOCACCIA BREAD WITH ROSEMARY

PESTO

LAYERED GOAT CHEESE TORTA WITH PESTO AND
SUN-DRIED TOMATOES

CRAB AND MUSHROOM PUFFS

BONED BREAST OF CHICKEN WITH BABY
VEGETABLES AND SOUR CREAM DILL SAUCE

CAESAR SALAD

CHOCOLATE DIPPED FRESH STRAWBERRIES

ALMOND TRUFFLES

WEDDING CAKE

Ryan proposed to Nina because she was pregnant with his child. At first, he was reluctant to marry, even though they had been living together for more than a year, because he was apprehensive about being a husband and father. While Nina's pregnancy developed, Ryan became excited about becoming a dad, and Nina was confident that he would make a good father because of the way he showed his love for her son, Phillip. Their quickly arranged wedding was attended by a select group of family and friends. Christine Blair, Nina's best friend, served as matron of honor, and Ryan's friend and supervisor, Neil Hastings, stood as best man. Several weeks into the marriage, however, Nina miscarried. She worried that Ryan would file for divorce, but he embraced their marriage. Ryan also suggested that he adopt Phillip.

CRUDITES WITH DIPPING SAUCE

7   large carrots
2   green bell peppers
2   red bell peppers
2   yellow bell peppers
5   bunches broccoli
2   cucumbers
4   yellow squash
2   zucchini
9   slices bacon
3   small tomatoes
1   8-ounce package cream cheese, softened
3   teaspoons prepared mustard
¼   teaspoon Tabasco sauce
1½   cups almonds
3   tablespoons green onion

■ Clean and julienne all vegetables into 2- to 3-inch strips. In a large skillet fry the bacon until crisp. Drain on paper towels, crumble, and set aside. In a food processor fitted with a steel blade combine the tomatoes, cream cheese, mustard, and Tabasco sauce. Add the almonds, onions, and bacon. Blend until the almonds are chopped. Refrigerate for 2 hours or up to 2 days. Serve with vegetables.
Serves 10 to 12.

FOCACCIA BREAD WITH ROSEMARY

DOUGH
1   tablespoon dry yeast
¼   cup water, 105° to 115°
     Pinch of sugar
2½   cups water
1   tablespoon olive oil
7   cups flour
1   teaspoon salt
2   tablespoons chopped fresh rosemary

TOPPING
2   tablespoons olive oil
2   teaspoons salt

■ Mix yeast with warm water and sugar. Let sit for 5 minutes, until foamy. Pour into a large mixing bowl, mixing with remaining water and olive oil. Mix in 1 cup of flour and salt. Add remaining flour 1 cup at a time. Knead for 8 minutes, until smooth and elastic. Add rosemary and knead until incorporated, about 1 more minute. Cover and permit to rise in a warm place for about 1 hour, or until doubled in volume. Punch down. Divide into thirds. Press with fingers into 3 lightly sprayed 9-inch cake pans. Let rise for 45 minutes. Dimple with fingertips. Cover with olive oil and sprinkle with salt. Let rise 45 minutes, until doubled in volume. Bake at 400°, throwing a handful of ice cubes on the oven floor to create steam (which makes a crisp crust). Bake for 20 minutes or until bread has a hollow sound when thumped. Remove bread from pans. Return to oven for 2 minutes to allow bottoms to crisp.
Makes 3 loaves.

PESTO

2 cups fresh basil
½ cup oil
⅓ cup piñon (pine) nuts
1 large clove garlic
1 teaspoon salt
½ teaspoon pepper
3 ounces Parmesan cheese

■ In a food processor combine the basil, oil, pine nuts, garlic, salt, and pepper. Pour into a bowl and stir in the cheese. Cover and refrigerate.
Makes 2 cups.

LAYERED GOAT CHEESE TORTA WITH PESTO AND SUN-DRIED TOMATOES

10 ounces goat cheese
2½ tablespoons virgin olive oil
½ tablespoon fresh lemon juice
2 to 4 prepared focaccia breads (see page 111 for focaccia recipe)
12 ounces prepared pesto sauce (see above for pesto recipe)
12 ounces thinly sliced prosciutto
2 12-ounce jars sun-dried tomatoes
Parsley for garnish

■ In a medium bowl mix the goat cheese, olive oil, and the lemon juice. Set aside. Spread a thin layer of pesto on the focaccia (any type of flat bread may be used). Cover the pesto with a layer of prosciutto. Spread a layer of the goat cheese mixture on top of the prosciutto. Add another thin layer of pesto. Top with drained sun-dried tomatoes. Cut into any size and shape and garnish with a sprig of parsley.
Serves 10 to 12.

CRAB AND MUSHROOM PUFFS

2¼ cups all-purpose flour
1½ cups warm water
¼ cup vegetable oil
1 teaspoon garlic powder
½ teaspoon salt
½ teaspoon black pepper
2 tablespoons Old Bay seasoning
½ pound backfin crabmeat
½ cup chopped scallions
½ cup finely chopped mushrooms
3 egg whites, whipped to stiff peaks
Peanut oil for frying
Cocktail sauce

■ In a small bowl combine flour, water, and vegetable oil with a wire whip. Combine with garlic powder, salt, pepper, and Old Bay seasoning. Gently add crab, scallions, and mushrooms and mix with a spoon. Fold in egg whites. Drop by medium spoonfuls into 350° peanut oil. Fry until firm or when a toothpick inserted in the center comes out dry. Drain. Serve with cocktail sauce.
Serves 6 to 8.

BONED BREAST OF CHICKEN WITH BABY VEGETABLES AND SOUR CREAM DILL SAUCE

Make the sauce in advance and chill. Serve as a side sauce to the warm chicken and vegetables. Fresh dill and a scattering of edible flowers make the presentation special.

SAUCE
1   tablespoon vegetable oil
2   shallots, minced
2   tablespoons minced chopped fresh dill
½   cup dry white wine
     Salt to taste
½   teaspoon ground white pepper
1   cup sour cream

CHICKEN
10   chicken breasts (6 ounces each), boneless and skinless
¼   cup flour
½   teaspoon salt
¼   cup vegetable oil

VEGETABLES
8   ounces baby carrots
8   ounces baby squashes (mixture of zucchini, summer, and patty pan)
8   ounces baby string beans

GARNISH
     Sprigs of fresh dill
     Edible flowers

■ For sauce, heat oil in a small skillet. Sauté shallots until wilted. Stir in dill, white wine, salt, and pepper. Cook over low heat until the liquid is reduced by half. Transfer to a glass dish and stir in sour cream. Refrigerate for at least 2 hours. Pound chicken to a uniform ½" thickness.

Dredge in a mixture of flour and salt. Sauté in a large skillet in vegetable oil for 2 minutes on each side until browned. Transfer to a roasting pan. Finish cooking the chicken at 350° for 12 to 15 minutes, until the interiors are no longer pink. Steam vegetables just until al dente. To serve, arrange warm chicken breast on each plate surrounded by vegetables. Garnish with a sprig of fresh dill. Pass the sauce separately.
Serves 10.

CAESAR SALAD

Enlightened Caesar dressing, for health reasons, no longer contains a raw egg, which is a boom to cholesterol watchers.

3   bunches romaine, deribbed, torn into bite-size pieces
2   cloves garlic, crushed
1   tablespoon anchovy paste
3   tablespoons apple cider vinegar
     Juice of 1 large lemon
1   teaspoon white Worcestershire sauce
½   teaspoon Dijon mustard
½   cup extra virgin olive oil
     Freshly grated pepper
1   cup herbed croutons
½   cup freshly shredded Parmesan cheese

■ In the bottom of a large wooden salad bowl, crush garlic with a fork. Mix in anchovy paste. Stir in vinegar, lemon juice, Worcestershire, and mustard. Vigorously stir in olive oil until all ingredients are incorporated and slightly thickened. Add lettuce. Toss until all leaves are coated. Grate pepper over salad. Add croutons and cheese. Toss and serve on chilled plates with chilled salad forks.
Serves 8.

CHOCOLATE DIPPED FRESH STRAWBERRIES

Could there possibly be anything more sensual or romantic than these giant strawberries at the peak of perfection dipped in bittersweet chocolate?

2 *dozen hand-selected, giant strawberries with stems attached*
3 *ounces semisweet chocolate*

■ Wash and drain strawberries. Melt chocolate in a large glass cup in the microwave or in the top of a double boiler. Dip each berry about halfway into the chocolate. Gently shake, permitting extra chocolate to fall back into the pan. Place on a waxpaper-lined cookie sheet and let chocolate harden, about 15 minutes at room temperature. These may be stored for several hours in the refrigerator before serving.

Note: Each 1-ounce square of chocolate will take about 2 minutes to melt in the microwave. Halfway through the cooking time, the chocolate should be stirred.
Makes 2 dozen.

ALMOND TRUFFLES

Victor Newman, an avowed ladies' man, has been known to send the finest truffles to his potential conquests—and to show up to share them at various times.

3 *squares semisweet chocolate*
4 *tablespoons butter, room temperature*
½ *cup confectioners' sugar*
1 *teaspoon almond extract*
2 *tablespoons finely chopped slivered almonds*

■ Melt chocolate in a large glass cup in the microwave or in the top of a double boiler. Stir in softened butter, sugar, and almond extract. With a measuring teaspoon, portion balls into 24 pieces. Place in refrigerator until partially hardened. With your hands, roll into round balls. Roll in almond pieces. Store in the refrigerator. Let soften slightly at room temperature before serving.

Note: Truffles like these may be frozen for several months.
Makes 2 dozen.

NIKKI AND JOSH

Menu

MARITA DELEON'S WHITE SUMMER SANGRIA

•

FRESH SWORDFISH STEAK WITH WATERMELON SALSA

•

ASHLEY JONES'S CHICKEN AND TOMATO OMELET

•

MELODY THOMAS SCOTT'S LAYERED SOUTHERN SALAD

•

SHARON CASE'S FRESH PEACHES AND
VANILLA ICE CREAM ANGEL CAKE

After a quick marriage in Las Vegas, Nikki and Josh stayed for a very brief honeymoon. Nikki's quick jaunt to Vegas with Josh was so troublesome for her son, Nick, that he flew to Kansas on the Newman jet to share the news with his father, Victor. Nick hoped that he and Victor might fly to Vegas and stop the wedding, but while the Newman jet was en route, the couple exchanged vows in a civil ceremony. Nikki hoped that her quick marriage and honeymoon would finally end the powerful feelings she had for Victor. After enjoying an intimate breakfast in their plush Vegas suite, Nikki and Josh returned to Genoa City, where her family struggled to accept the new marriage.

MARITA DELEON'S WHITE SUMMER SANGRIA

Serve this citrusy, white sangria from a large pitcher for an elegant, refreshing summer drink.

⅓   cup fresh lemon juice
⅓   cup fresh lime juice
1   cup fresh orange juice
1   cup seltzer, club soda, or sparkling mineral water
1½   cups ginger ale
1   bottle (750 ml.) dry white wine, chilled
½   cup Pimm's Cup (English liqueur)
1   navel orange, cut into wedges
1   lemon, cut into wedges

■ In a large pitcher stir together citrus juices, seltzer (or soda or mineral water), ginger ale, wine, Pimm's Cup, and ½ the orange and lemon wedges. Add ice. Pour into 6 glasses and garnish with remaining orange and lemon wedges. *Serves 6.*

FRESH SWORDFISH STEAK WITH WATERMELON SALSA

Do not prepare this dish unless you want to earn a reputation as an inventive cook. And do not even think about trying this with anything except impeccably fresh swordfish and ripe, juicy watermelon.

4   swordfish steaks (about 6 ounces each)
2   cups watermelon pieces, bite-sized chunks
2   tablespoons thinly sliced garlic chives (or substitute scallions)
2   tablespoons red wine vinegar
½   teaspoon ground chili powder
½   teaspoon salt
    Garlic chives for garnish

■ Broil swordfish about 2 minutes on each side. The fish should be just warmed in the center. For salsa, remove seeds from watermelon. In a medium bowl combine watermelon, chives, vinegar, chili powder, and salt. Spoon salsa onto 4 plates. Top with fish. Garnish with garlic chives.

Note: If the watermelon lacks sweetness, add 1 to 2 teaspoons sugar to the salsa. *Serves 4.*

ASHLEY JONES'S CHICKEN AND TOMATO OMELET

This omelet with robust flavors can be whipped up in less than 10 minutes.

1   tablespoon butter
2   eggs, beaten
¼   cup chopped, cooked chicken meat
1   roma tomato, seeded and chopped
1   teaspoon chopped fresh basil, optional
      Salt and pepper to taste

■ In a 7-inch skillet heat butter over medium heat. Pour in eggs. Stir with a fork for several seconds. As omelet starts to set, lift edges gently with fork, permitting uncooked eggs to slide underneath and cook. When most of the egg is cooked, sprinkle with chicken, tomato, optional basil, salt, and pepper. Let cook for several more minutes. With a spatula lift top half of omelet and fold over. Flip onto a warm plate.

Note: A nonstick skillet makes preparation quite simple. All butter can be eliminated if the skillet is sprayed with vegetable oil.
Serves 1.

MELODY THOMAS SCOTT'S LAYERED SOUTHERN SALAD

1   head iceberg lettuce
4   green onions, chopped
2   5-ounce cans sliced water
      chestnuts, drained
4   ribs celery, chopped
1   10-ounce package frozen peas
1   cup mayonnaise (cold-pressed suggested)
1   tablespoon sugar
8   slices crisp bacon, crumbled
3   hard-boiled eggs, sliced
8   ounces cheddar cheese

■ Individually layer in a large bowl lettuce followed by onions, water chestnuts, celery, and peas. Slather mayonnaise on top of the

peas. Sprinkle with sugar. Cover with plastic wrap. Refrigerate overnight. Just before serving, top with bacon, eggs, and cheese. Toss each serving separately.
Serves 6.

SHARON CASE'S FRESH PEACHES AND VANILLA ICE CREAM ANGEL CAKE

Sharon Case loves peaches and vanilla ice cream. Make this when fresh peaches are fragrantly ripe. Buy the round angel food cake with the center hole, which is readily available in the supermarket. Let ice cream soften for 5 to 10 minutes at room temperature before using.

8   *large fresh peaches, peeled and sliced*
3   *tablespoons sugar*
    Juice of 1 lemon
1   *angel food cake*
1   *quart vanilla ice cream, premium quality*
    Sprigs of fresh mint for garnish

■ Slice peaches into a bowl. Stir in sugar and lemon juice. Let sit for 10 minutes. Slice angel cake horizontally in half. Spread bottom half of cake with ice cream. Spread half the peaches on top. Replace top half of cake. Pour peach juices onto the cake. Arrange peach slices on top. Garnish with sprigs of fresh mint. The cake may be held in the freezer covered with wax paper for about 20 minutes. Be very careful not to freeze the peaches.

Note: The bottom half of the cake spread with ice cream can be prepared in advance and stored in the freezer. The peaches can be prepared with sugar and lemon and stored in the refrigerator. Just before serving, assemble, adding peaches and the remainder of the cake.

Serves 10.

Nikki and Victoria were both filled with joy moments before Nikki's wedding ceremony to Brad was about to begin. Their happiness was shattered when word reached them that Victor had been shot in his office.

CHRIS AND PAUL

Menu

LIME-MARINATED GRILLED PRAWNS

JAMES IVY'S LEMON-HERBED ROASTED CHICKEN

ARUGULA AND CUCUMBER SAUTÉED WITH
HONEY DIJON MUSTARD

TOASTED BROWN RICE AND SUNFLOWER SEEDS

HONEYDEW ICE

Newlywed Chris was concluding some last-minute business in Denver for Newman Enterprises when her husband, Paul, called with an enticing proposition. Instead of returning to Genoa City, he asked that she meet him in Nevis. After weeks of postponing their honeymoon because of heavy work schedules, Chris and Paul were finally able to celebrate their marriage. The balmy, sun-filled Caribbean island was the perfect background for romantic adventures, including golf, tennis, sightseeing, and candlelit dinners. Unfortunately, their honeymoon was nearly destroyed by Phyllis Romalotti, who had won a trip to the island in a contest. Phyllis did her best to harass Paul and Chris with nasty pranks, including crawling into bed with an unsuspecting Paul. Her cruel tricks came to an abrupt end when Chris and Paul discovered that she was the mastermind behind their misadventures. Phyllis promptly left the island with her companion, Dr. Tim Reid, leaving the couple to enjoy their honeymoon in blissful peace.

JAMES IVY'S LEMON-HERBED ROASTED CHICKEN

"I like a lemon taste. I like variety. I like it usually with a lemon herb brushed on the skin. I usually pull the skin off, but the flavor soaks in." Served with his mother's mashed potatoes, this is his favorite dish. Starting the chicken upside down helps keep the breast moist.

3½ *pounds whole chicken*
1 *tablespoon butter, melted*
  Juice and zest of 1 lemon
2 *tablespoons dried, crushed herbs de Provence (mixture of basil, fennel, lavender, marjoram, thyme, sage, rosemary)*
½ *teaspoon crushed black pepper*

■ Clean chicken and pull off any excess fat. Mix melted butter with lemon juice and zest, herbs and pepper. Rub spice mixture on the skin and on the interior cavity. Place breast side down on a rack sprayed with vegetable oil in a roasting pan. Roast at 400° for 45 minutes, basting with pan juices after 15 minutes. Turn chicken over. Baste with pan juices every 15 minutes. Continue to roast until the juices run clear and the dark meat is fully cooked, 45 to 60 minutes.
Serves 4.

ARUGULA AND CUCUMBER SAUTÉED WITH HONEY DIJON MUSTARD

The bitterness of the arugula greens contrasted with the sweet honey and tangy mustard makes this a wonderful accompaniment to most any meal. Even the humble cucumber gets its deserved minute of fame. Cooked without its seeds, the cucumber takes on a startling transformation.

2 *tablespoons olive oil*
1 *large cucumber, peeled, seeded, and cut into ½-inch moon slices*
¼ *cup Dijon mustard*
¼ *cup honey*
½ *teaspoon salt*
½ *teaspoon freshly ground black pepper*
½ *pound arugula, washed*

■ In a large skillet heat olive oil. Sauté cucumber until wilted, about 2 minutes. Stir in mustard, honey, salt, and pepper. Reduce heat to low. Place arugula on top. Cover until arugula starts to lose its crispness, about 2 minutes. Stir all ingredients together to fully coat the vegetables with the sauce.
Serves 4.

TOASTED BROWN RICE AND SUNFLOWER SEEDS

Pan-toasting brown rice and sunflower seeds adds a new taste dimension. And brown rice still has the nutritious coating and fiber that has been robbed from the white version.

1½ tablespoons vegetable oil
1 cup long-grain brown rice
⅓ cup sunflower seeds
2 cups chicken stock
1 teaspoon salt

■ In a medium skillet heat oil. Toast rice and sunflower seeds over medium heat for 10 minutes or until browned. Transfer to a medium pan. Add stock and salt. Bring to a boil. Reduce heat. Cover. Cook until the grains have absorbed the liquid, 35 to 40 minutes.
Serves 4.

HONEYDEW ICE

Pale green, minty crystals cool hot taste buds during the summer season. This is not a fine-textured ice. It is made directly in the freezer with no other special equipment.

3 cups cubed, honeydew melon
1 small bunch fresh mint
¼ cup sugar
¼ cup water

■ In a food processor, puree melon and mint. In a small pan over medium heat dissolve sugar in water. Cool. Mix with fruit. Pour into a 13x9x2-inch metal baking pan. Place in freezer. Every 10 minutes scrape ice crystals from the edge of the pan. Continue this procedure for about 1 hour or until a uniformly icy product is formed. Serve immediately.
Note: Try this with other fruits, adjusting the quantity of sugar to taste.
Serves 6.

Chris and Paul enjoy a romantic honeymoon feast on the sandy beaches of Nevis.

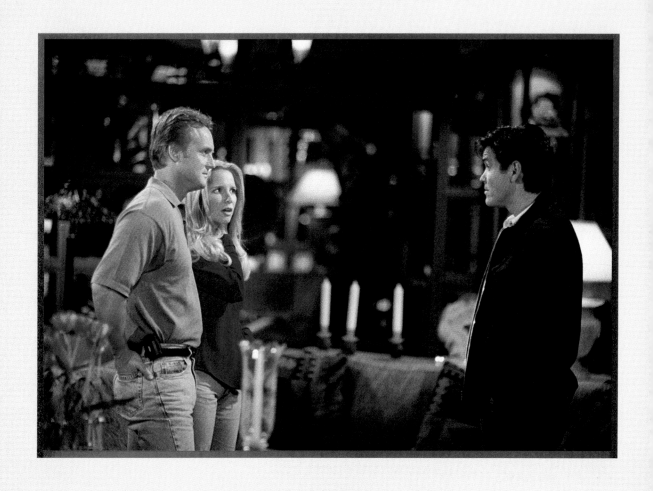

Comfort Foods for Devastating Breakups

Breaking up is hard to do. When a relationship ends, whether it ends explosively or just fizzles out, both people can feel devastated. At times like that, sometimes the only relief can be found in comfort foods, something to ease the sting of lost romance, something to munch on when the hurt just gets worse, or something to chew on while revenge tantalizes the mind of one who feels scorned. Comfort foods are not limited to breakups, however. A good munchie is a good munchie regardless of whether one has been foiled, fouled, or frustrated.

HUEVOS RANCHEROS

Olé! Life can be great when the morning contains Miquel Rodriquez's Mexican-style ranch eggs. He likes breakfast to be hearty and includes a large serving of refried beans covered with a mild, locally made fresh Mexican cheese. And to satisfy his heat seekers, there is always a bottle of hot sauce within arm's reach.

8	*corn tortillas*
2	*tablespoons vegetable oil*
2	*onions, sliced*
3	*tomatoes, chopped*
2	*teaspoons ground red chili powder*
½	*teaspoon salt*
¼	*teaspoon ground oregano*
8	*eggs*

■ Wrap tortillas in aluminum foil. Heat in a 350° oven for 10 to 12 minutes. In a large skillet heat oil. Cook onions until wilted. Stir in tomatoes, chili powder, salt, and oregano. Crack eggs into sauce, being careful not to break the yolks. Reduce heat to low. Cover and cook until the yolks reach the desired consistency. Place two tortillas on each plate. Cover each with an egg and top with the ranchero sauce.
Serves 4.

GENOA CITY NO-WOES FRUIT AND CHOCOLATE MIX

This rich mix is like a box of fruit and nut dark chocolates with the goodies exposed. And sometimes life is a bit easier without the mysteries in the assorted box.

1	*cup semisweet chocolate chips*
½	*cup toasted almond slivers*
½	*cup toasted macadamia nuts*
½	*cup toasted pecans*
½	*cup sun-dried cherries*
½	*cup sun-dried blueberries*
½	*cup sun-dried strawberries*

■ Toss all ingredients together. Store in an airtight, easy-to-find location. And eat to get rid of woes.
Makes 4 cups.

AUTUMN'S GOLDEN BUTTERNUT SQUASH AND APPLE SOUP

Butternut squash and apples are the quintessential reminder of the crisp days of fall. And the golden color of this soup mirrors the golden hues of the season's leaves.

1	*small butternut squash*
1	*tablespoon olive oil*
1	*onion, chopped*
2	*cups chicken broth*
2	*tart apples, cored and chopped*
2	*large carrots, peeled and chopped*
1	*cup milk*
1	*teaspoon salt*
1/4	*teaspoon ground nutmeg*

■ Wash squash. Cut in half. Remove and discard seeds. Place squash in a medium pot and cover with 1 inch of water. Boil squash for 15 minutes or until flesh softens. Drain squash. With a spoon scrape squash from shell. In a soup pot, heat olive oil. Sauté onion over medium heat until translucent or for 5 minutes. Add chicken broth, apples, and carrots. Simmer for 20 to 30 minutes or until all vegetables are tender. Transfer to a food processor or blender. Process until smooth. Return to pot. Add milk and seasonings. Heat and serve.

Note: Squash may also be quickly prepared in the microwave. This might be preferable as the flavor will be concentrated.

Serves 4 to 6.

Although Nikki and Victor are no longer married, they continue to share a special bond. They see each other on a regular basis, including holiday parties.

HERBED TURKEY MEAT LOAVES

Ground turkey has become the darling of Genoa City residences striving for lower cholesterol, fewer calories, and inexpensive protein sources. Esther Valentine, the maid for Katherine Chancellor, delights her charges with this nutritional twist on the American classic ground-beef loaves. She often changes the seasonings and finds that barbecue sauce or salsa brushed on the loaves about 5 minutes before the end of the cooking time makes quite a hit.

1⅓	*pounds lean, ground turkey*
⅓	*cup oats, old fashioned*
1	*medium onion, chopped*
1	*egg, beaten*
1	*teaspoon Italian herbs, dried*
1	*teaspoon salt*
½	*teaspoon ground black pepper*
½	*teaspoon chili flakes*

■ Mix turkey, oats, onion, egg, herbs, salt, pepper, and chili lightly with a fork. Divide into 6 portions. Place in a muffin tin sprayed with vegetable oil. Slightly flatten each top so that the meat takes on the shape of the tin. Bake in a 350° oven for 20 to 25 minutes or until the centers are no longer pink.

Note: For free-form shapes fashion into giant meatballs and bake in a 13x9x2-inch pan sprayed with vegetable oil. The children like these shaped into dinosaurs. "We ate dinosaur for dinner," they brag.

Makes 6 loaves.

Nikki and Victor

Although Nikki and Victor are no longer married, they have a special bond, primarily because of their children, Victoria and Nicholas. Each has tremendous respect for the other's parenting skills, but the affection Nikki and Victor feel toward each other is not based exclusively on their children; it also stems from the dramatic obstacles they have overcome together. Victor's love for Nikki is so strong that he has heroically risked his own life for her in life-threatening situations. Nikki graciously credits Victor's refined taste with broadening her own interests, which have helped her to grow into one of the most highly regarded women in Genoa City. Meanwhile, Nikki's sensitivity has helped Victor to better express himself emotionally, which has had a profound effect on his relationship with his children.

Victoria and Ryan

An underage Victoria Newman was so hell-bent on marrying Ryan McNeil that she did so without telling her parents, Victor and Nikki. Shortly after the marriage, Victoria and Ryan discovered that her basic sense of insecurity had made her frigid. Part of the problem stemmed from Ryan's ongoing affair with Nina Webster, who was older and much more worldly than Victoria, who had grown up in a boarding school, sheltered from the real world. Eventually, Victoria accepted that the problems in her marriage could not be solved. To her dismay, Ryan agreed with her. Feeling humiliated, she packed her bags and moved in with her mother, Nikki. Soon after, Victoria divorced Ryan. Since then, she and Ryan have developed an extremely close and trusting relationship. On several occasions they have flirted with the idea of resuming their romance, but before losing control of their passions, either one or the other has realized the eventual dire consequences of an affair.

SALMON, LEEK, AND POTATO SOUP

This hearty soup, thickened with potatoes and enlivened with the sweet taste of leeks, is swimming with fresh salmon. Just think of all the healthy omega-3 fatty acids in each bowlful. Ask the fish monger for the odd pieces of boneless fillets for soup. Often they are less expensive.

$\frac{2}{3}$ **pound salmon fillets**
2 **pounds potatoes, peeled and cut into chunks**
1 **large leek, chopped**
4 **cups water**
1 **bay leaf**
2 **teaspoons salt**
$\frac{1}{2}$ **teaspoon black pepper**

■ Remove any bones remaining in the salmon. Place salmon, potatoes, leek, water, and bay leaf in a large soup pot. Bring to a boil. Reduce heat and simmer for about 1 hour or until thickened. Remove bay leaf. Add salt and pepper. Serve piping hot.
Serves 8.

JAMAICAN JERK PORK TENDERLOIN

No, jerks are not the misbehaving boy-friends; they are a mixture of tantalizing spices and the hotness from habeñeros, the hottest pepper on this earth. The Jamaicans have turned jerk rubs into an art form. Here we have substituted the jalapeño pepper, which is not as hot but is certainly worthy of respect. Allspice, called pimento in Jamaica, adds an unusual sweetness. Serve with baked plantains, rice, and lots of icy, cold beverages.

> 2   *pork tenderloins (about 2 pounds)*
> 1   *medium onion, peeled and quartered*
> 2 to 4 *jalapeño peppers, seeded,*
>   *with ribs removed*
> ½   *teaspoon ground allspice*
> ½   *teaspoon salt*
> ¼   *teaspoon ground cinnamon*
> ¼   *teaspoon ground nutmeg*

■ Trim tenderloins of all fat and silver skin. In a food processor puree jalapeños, onion, allspice, salt, cinnamon, and nutmeg for the jerk. Rub the jerk sauce on the meat. Refrigerate for an hour or so before grilling. Grill about 4 inches above medium hot coals for 10 minutes on each side, until the inside is still pink and a meat ther-mometer registers an internal temperature of 155°. Permit to sit for 10 minutes so that the juices can distribute. Cut into ½-inch slices on the diagonal.

Note: The original jerked foods were barbe-cued on the northeastern coast of Jamaica at Boston Beach. Today visitors can sit at delightful outdoor shacks and order jerked pork, beef, chicken, and even lobster, with cans of icy beer.

Serves 6.

KRISTOFF ST. JOHN'S ULTIMATE PB&J

Kristoff St. John has shared his secret for the grown-up PB&J on a toasted English muffin. Try both ver-sions—either with the classic sliced banana or with more crunch from toasted sunflower seeds. To feed a whole cast of characters, toast muffins under the broiler.

> 2   *whole-wheat English muffins*
> 3   *tablespoons crunchy peanut butter*
> 2   *tablespoons strawberry preserves*
> 1   *small banana, peeled and sliced, or 2*
>   *tablespoons toasted sunflower seeds*

■ Fork split English muffins to create the little crannies. Toast until golden brown. Spread with peanut butter and preserves. Top with choice of banana or sunflower seeds.
Serves 2.

YUKON GOLD MASHED POTATOES

We will refrain from mentioning the name, but one housekeeper did the unthinkable. She put black pepper into the mashed potatoes. Everyone tried to figure out the nature of those dirty specks. Fortunately, she was discretely informed to use only white pepper in mashed potatoes. Later she discovered these golden Yukons, and her former indiscretions were forever forgotten. Now famous, she is very, very secure in her position.

6 medium Yukon Gold potatoes, peeled, quartered, and boiled until soft
½ cup milk
1 teaspoon salt
½ teaspoon ground white pepper
2 tablespoons butter

■ Use an old-fashioned potato masher with an up-and-down movement to incorporate air while mashing. Gradually add milk, continuing with the up-and-down movement. Stir in salt and white pepper. Dot with butter. Serve warm.
Serves 4.

Katherine, who was once married to Danny's deceased father, Rex Sterling, continues to have an interest in Danny's well-being.

BAKED HALIBUT STEAKS IN SOUR CREAM WITH RED EMPEROR GRAPES

The seedless Red Emperor grapes have a crisp, sweet taste. These grapes, paired with meaty halibut in a light sour cream and white wine sauce, make a delightful entrée. Serve with steamed rice.

1¼ *pounds halibut steaks (4 pieces)*
1 *cup fresh Red Emperor grapes, halved*
½ *cup sour cream*
2 *tablespoons dry white wine*
1 *teaspoon salt*
¼ *teaspoon ground white pepper*
Fresh Red Emperor grapes for garnish

■ Place halibut in a small ovenproof dish. Cover with grapes. Mix sour cream, white wine, salt, and pepper in a small dish. Spoon over grapes. Bake at 350° for 20 to 30 minutes or until the fish is almost opaque in the center. Garnish with fresh grapes.

Note: Be careful not to overcook the fish. Overcooking results in a loss of moisture. Shorter baking time is required for thinner steaks. The fish is done *before* it begins to flake. *Serves 4.*

Christine and Danny

When Danny Romalotti received the wonderful news that he'd been cast as the lead in a Broadway musical, he did not realize that it would generate irreparable damage to his marriage to Chris. Danny wanted her to join him in New York City, but a blossoming legal career prevented her making the trip. Several months later, she received a letter from Danny in which he said that he wanted a divorce. In the ensuing days, Chris experienced a roller coaster of emotions, including confusion, shock, and finally, heartbreak. Chris understood there were problems in her marriage to Danny, but she could not fathom why he would want a divorce rather than try to work out their problems. Months later, she finally learned the truth. When Danny's new wife, Phyllis, arrived in Genoa City carrying a newborn infant and introduced herself as the mother of Danny's son, Daniel Romalotti.

GRANVILLE "SONNY" VAN DUSEN'S PENNE ARRABBIATA

Sonny gave the following directions for this spicy pasta dish: "You take Italian skinned tomatoes—Progresso makes great skinned tomatoes—about a pound. Reduce them and make the sauce thick. Meanwhile, in another pan, [add] olive oil for the bottom of the pan. I cut up garlic (four cloves), red pepper, red-hot chili peppers that are dried. Break them up; test on your tongue. If it burns, use less. I usually use 2 or 3. I put that with the garlic, salt, and pepper in the olive oil. Brown the garlic. When the garlic starts to turn brown, turn off the heat. Put in the tomatoes when the garlic and olive oil mixture is cooled. Let simmer for 45 minutes. If the tomatoes have been chopped ahead of time, it won't take as long. Add ¼ cup of red wine to it. It helps combine the flavor of the olive oil and tomatoes. Then you cook the penne until it's al dente. Toss it all together in a big bowl. I don't use cheese, but you can use a Romano, just not very much; it takes away the flavor and heat. It should be very spicy."

1	15-ounce can skinned, diced tomatoes
2	tablespoons olive oil
4	cloves garlic, sliced
2 or 3	dried red chili peppers, broken up
	Salt and pepper to taste
¼	cup red wine
1	pound penne pasta

■ In a small saucepan reduce tomatoes with their juices to a thick sauce. In a separate skillet heat olive oil. Sauté garlic until it begins to brown. Stir in hot peppers and salt and pepper to taste. Turn off heat and let cool. Add tomatoes and red wine to skillet. Simmer until a thick sauce consistency is reached, about 35 to 45 minutes. Cook penne in a large quantity of water until al dente. Drain. In a large bowl toss pasta with sauce. Serve immediately.
Serves 4.

INDIAN BASMATI RICE WITH RAISINS AND SLIVERED ALMONDS

Basmati rice, grown at the base of the Himalayan Mountains, is one of the most fragrant rices. Unlike domestic rices, it should be rinsed before cooking to remove excess starch.

1	cup basmati rice
1¾	cups chicken stock or water
2	tablespoons raisins
2	tablespoons slivered almonds
1	teaspoon salt

■ Rinse rice to remove excess starch. In a heavy pot bring all ingredients to a boil. Reduce to a simmer. Cook covered until all the moisture is absorbed and the grains are tender, about 25 to 30 minutes.
Serves 4.

ROASTED SWEET ONIONS WITH TARRAGON

This is simply not one of those items for "share-seys." The first bite of these sensual, slippery, and sweet roasted onions makes one lose all inhibitions, and no one is inclined to give any away. Make sure that any and all negotiations are completed before serving them. If that fails, use these to up the ante. These are not exactly finger foods, so be very cautious of any and all flying forks.

6   *large supersweet onions (Vidalia, Maui, Granex, Walla Walla), peeled*
2   *tablespoons freshly chopped tarragon (or substitute 1 teaspoon dried)*
2   *tablespoons olive oil*
½   *teaspoon salt*
    Freshly ground black pepper

■ With a small paring knife, remove about 2 inches of the top onion stem. Arrange onions, tops up, in a ceramic or glass baking dish. Sprinkle with tarragon. Drizzle with olive oil. Season with salt and pepper. Bake at 400° for 50 to 60 minutes or until they are tender.
Serves 6 (perhaps).

Danny and Phyllis

From the early days of Phyllis's involvement with Danny Romalotti, she has harbored a dark secret: The child she claimed as Danny's was fathered by another man. Nevertheless, she has gone to great lengths to make Danny believe he was Daniel's father. One such ploy included slipping him a potent drink that caused Danny to black out and believe that he might have made love to Phyllis, which led to her pregnancy. She has also altered blood test results at the lab where she once worked to make it look like Danny was Daniel's father, eventually submitting to blackmail by her former friend, Sasha Greene, and stealing blood from the real father and passing it off as Danny's. In the end, with the help of Danny's former wife, Chris, and Chris's husband, Paul Williams, Danny finally discovered the truth. Feeling betrayed by Phyllis's devious behavior, he resolved to cut all ties with her completely, but at the same time he had become so attached to Daniel that he continued to play the role of father to the young boy.

FAST DINNER SOLUTION FOR A HAPPY FAMILY

For the working mothers in Genoa City coming home to children screaming, "Mom, I am starving to death!" here is a fabulous and cheap skillet dish. Brown the onion and ground turkey at warp speed. Toss some chopped Savoy cabbage and a diced tomato on top. Cover and let it do its own thing while the children get attention. Add some cheese, American for the children or some-thing with more flavor for others. Relax and enjoy a slice of family life. For the kids, this meal is healthier and FASTER than fast food and will taste good will all kinds of alterations. If a child is nearby have him or her wash and poke with a fork 4 potatoes and zap them in the microwave. They will be done at the same time as the skillet dinner. Nothing tastes better than dinner lovingly cooked by Mom.

> ½ onion, roughly chopped
> 1 pound ground turkey
> 1 tablespoon Worcestershire sauce
> 1 teaspoon salt
> ½ head Savoy cabbage
> 1 Roma tomato, chopped
> Grated cheese

■ Place heavy skillet on burner turned to high. Spray with vegetable oil. Toss in chopped onion. Unwrap ground turkey. Smash it down into the skillet, touching only the wrapping paper. Keep the temperature on high. Turn on the exhaust fan. Take a deep breath. Douse on the Worces-tershire sauce and salt. Take a spatula and stir up skillet contents. Toss with reckless abandon.

Keep the heat on high. Chop the cabbage. When turkey is no longer pink, dump cabbage and tomato on top of meat. Turn down heat. Cover pan. Take 5. Smile at the children. Change your clothes. Smile. Add cheese to skillet and take it to the table. Serve. Smile. You did it, and it tastes great. Ask your fans for confirmation.
Serves 4.

HERBED GARLIC PITA TOASTS

Whole-grain pita pocket breads make a ter-rific snack. Their transformation with butter, garlic, and herbs is amazing . . . and so easy. Serve with Italian Herbed Chickpea Dip (page 26), Cumin Eggplant Dip with Pita Triangles (page 55), or all by themselves.

> 4 whole-grain pita breads
> 3 tablespoons butter
> 2 cloves garlic, pressed
> 1 teaspoon Italian herbs, dried
> ½ teaspoon salt

■ Open each pita bread. In a small pan over low heat, melt butter with garlic, herbs, and salt. Using a pastry brush, coat the inside of each pita with the melted butter mixture. Cut each pita half into 6 pieces. Place on a baking sheet but-tered side up. Bake at 325° for 15 minutes or until browned. Serve immediately.
Serves 4.

PANFRIED CHUNKY RUSSET POTATOES

Potatoes are possibly the most traditional American side dish. Russets, which are a mealy textured potato, make delicious panfried potatoes. Cut the potatoes into chunks approximately 2-inches thick and sauté over high heat in a skillet. These make an excellent accompaniment for breakfast eggs or for stuffing inside a breakfast burrito.

2	tablespoons vegetable oil
2	cloves garlic, minced
4	baking potatoes, cut into 2-inch chunks
1	teaspoon salt
½	teaspoon pepper
¼	teaspoon paprika

■ In a large skillet heat oil. Sauté garlic until golden, about 3 minutes. Add potatoes. Toss occasionally. Cook until the potatoes have a crisp exterior and tender interior, about 15 minutes. Season with salt, pepper, and paprika.

Note: To shorten preparation time, first microwave potatoes for several minutes. Then cut into chunks and begin the stovetop panfrying.
Serves 4.

Jill and John

When John Abbott suffered a temporary bout of impotency, a Pandora's box of troubles opened in his marriage to Jill. She finally turned to contractor Jed Sanders for gratification, but their affair was discovered by John's longtime housekeeper, Mamie, who always felt Jill was wrong for her boss. Eventually, Mamie exposed the affair to John, who became enraged and filed for divorce. The courtroom became an ugly battleground for the custody of their son, Billy. The constant stress of the custody fight caused John to suffer a stroke, and he temporarily lost his memory, forgetting that Jill had cheated on him. His loss of memory was brief, and the custody battle was rejoined. It was resolved by having Jill remain in residence at the Abbott mansion, and she and John shared custody, but they no longer lived as husband and wife.

BAKED SPAGHETTI SQUASH ACCENTED WITH TARRAGON AND HONEY

This is such a fun squash to prepare and eat. The squash is cut and the seeds removed before baking. Then mix with honey, butter, and tarragon.

1   *spaghetti squash, about 2 pounds*
1   *tablespoon honey*
1   *tablespoon butter, optional*
2   *teaspoons fresh, chopped tarragon (substitute ¾ teaspoon dried)*
1   *teaspoon salt*
½   *teaspoon pepper*

■ Cut squash in half lengthwise. Scoop out seeds with a large metal spoon. Place cut side up in a large casserole dish with ¼ inch of water outside the squash. Cover with foil. Bake at 350° until tender but not soft, about 40 minutes. With a fork gently pull out strands. Place in a serving dish. Toss with honey, optional butter, tarragon, salt, and pepper.

Note: The entire squash can also be cooked in the microwave. Pierce first and follow manufacturer's timing suggestions.

Serves 6.

John, who was concerned for his son Billy's welfare, confronts Keith after Jill moved into Keith's home with Billy.

SMOKED GOUDA FLAKY BISCUIT DIAMONDS

Biscuits have been an American tradition for centuries. Recipes like this one have been handed down through the generations. The secret is to handle the dough gently just like a family heirloom and to be sure that it is sufficiently wet. In the Abbott family, a favorite signature is the smoked Gouda.

2	*cups flour*
2	*teaspoons baking powder*
1	*teaspoon salt*
½	*teaspoon baking soda*
5	*tablespoons butter*
¾	*cup buttermilk*
¼	*cup chopped smoked Gouda cheese*
1	*tablespoon buttermilk, for brushing tops*

■ Mix flour, baking powder, salt, and baking soda in a medium bowl. With a fork, cut in butter. Quickly stir in buttermilk and Gouda. Transfer to a lightly floured pastry board. Knead just to incorporate all ingredients. Roll to ¼ inch. Cut into diamonds. Brush the tops with buttermilk. Bake at 425° until the tops are golden brown, for 12 to 15 minutes.
Makes 2 dozen biscuits.

CHUNKY PEANUT BUTTER AND STRAWBERRY JAM MUFFINS

This little muffin guarantees to take one back to the comfort of childhood. The subtle taste of peanut butter is perfectly matched to a sweet, sticky jam center. The texture is superb, and the fear of peanut butter stuck to the roof of the mouth or, even worse, to one's braces, is eliminated. Warning: Those little people still in their first childhood will also quickly embrace these muffins, which taste just as comforting warm as cool.

⅓	*cup chunky peanut butter*
2	*tablespoons vegetable oil*
1	*egg*
2	*tablespoons sugar*
1	*cup milk*
2	*cups flour*
2	*teaspoons baking powder*
½	*teaspoon salt*
¼	*cup strawberry jam*

■ In a medium mixing bowl combine peanut butter and oil. Stir in egg, sugar, and milk. Add flour, baking powder and salt. Quickly mix until just incorporated. Spoon into greased muffin tins. Drop 1 teaspoon jam into center of each muffin. Bake at 400° for 20 minutes, until the tops are golden.
Makes 12 muffins.

SCOTT REEVES'S FAT-FREE TURKEY LASAGNA

For those big family gatherings you will want to use three large rectangular pans. For smaller gatherings, you may want to divide everything by three.

4½ pounds of ground turkey
9 cloves minced garlic
5 6-ounce cans tomato paste
4½ 20-ounce cans tomatoes
4½ teaspoons salt
3⅜ teaspoons pepper
4½ teaspoons oregeno
27 prepared lasgna noodles (boiled)
36 ounces fat-free mozarella cheese
54 ounces fat-free ricotta cheese

■ Brown turkey and garlic together. Add tomato paste, tomatoes, and seasonings. Cover and simmer for 20 minutes. Layer prepared noodles, cheeses, and prepared turkey sauce in a pan in the following order: sauce, noodles, mozarella cheese, and ricotta cheese. Make four layers. Preheat oven to 350°. Bake 20 to 30 minutes, or until hot and bubbly.
Serves 25.

BRAISED PORK LOIN WITH TART APPLES AND BROWN LENTILS

Lentils are the perfect designer pantry food, particularly in a state that may average more than 45 inches of snowfall annually. As no soaking is required, lentils get pedestal status with cooking time equal to about half *The Young and the Restless's* airing time. Serve with a crisp green salad.

1 tablespoon oil
2 cloves garlic, minced
1 pound lean pork loin, cut into 1-inch cubes
1 cup brown lentils, washed and picked over
2 cups apple cider
1 tart cooking apple (such as Granny Smith), cored and chopped
2 whole, fresh sage leaves, crushed (or substitute ½ teaspoon ground sage)
1½ teaspoons salt
1 teaspoon black pepper

■ In a large pot sauté in oil the garlic and pork pieces for 2 minutes. Reduce heat. Add lentils, cider, apple, and sage. Cover and cook until the lentils are tender, about 30 minutes. Add salt and pepper.
Serves 4.

VEGETARIAN CHILI

Make up a huge pot for big events. Keep it simmering on the stove until the hunger urge strikes. Serve with bowls of fresh salsa, cheese, and grated onions for condiments.

1   pound dried pinto beans
1   tablespoon oil
2   large onions, chopped
4   cloves garlic, minced
1   28-ounce can diced tomatoes in puree
1   16-ounce can corn kernels with juices
1   green pepper, chopped
2   tablespoons chili powder
1   tablespoon cocoa powder
4 to 6 cups water
    Salt and pepper to taste

■ Clean beans. Place in a large bowl and cover with 3 inches of water. Soak overnight. Drain. Heat oil in a large soup pot. Sauté onions and garlic until translucent, about 5 minutes. Stir in tomatoes, corn, green peppers, chili powder, and cocoa powder. Add soaked beans and 4 cups of water. Bring to a boil. Stir. Reduce heat to a simmer. Cover and cook for 1 to 2 hours or until the beans are tender. Add additional water as needed. Add salt and pepper to taste.
Serves 8 to 10.

CHOCOLATE AND FRUIT FONDUE FANTASY

The children at Katherine Chancellor's pool parties are frequently often treated to this chocolate construction kit. This is a kid's chocolate fantasy with some of their favorite fruits. Outside is the only safe place to truly enjoy this fondue, with no fear of spilling on Oriental carpets or marring fine antique furniture.

1   12-ounce package chocolate chips
½   cup evaporated milk
½   cup sugar
2   cups strawberries, hulled
2   bananas, sliced
1   cup seedless green grapes
1   apple, sliced
    Angel food cake, small chunks

■ In a heavy pan over low heat, melt chocolate chips. Gradually stir in milk and sugar. Transfer to a fondue pot. Ignite heat source. Keep heat very low. Present with a large platter of the fruits and cake. Pass long-handled fondue forks for dipping and lots of napkins.
Serves 6.

Cravings

Unusual cravings are an "expected" part of pregnancy, and they affect both mom and dad and sometimes uncles and aunts and grandparents. Whether pregnant or not (and sometimes that's worth celebrating), everyone loves to indulge in the pursuit of exciting new taste treats. Here are salty snacks and sweet delights to satisfy the full spectrum of cravings, but at all times the spirit of satisfying those cravings should be one of indulgence! The Young and the Restless *has its full share of little surprises and welcome additions.*

BREAKFAST CHEESECAKE WITH FRESH FRUIT

Cheesecake for breakfast is certainly not neurotic. The idea, once examined, has substantial merit. This one is made with nonfat cream cheese of primarily skim milk containing protein, some carbohydrates, and some calcium—and, of course, no fat grams. Next, it is made to look like muffins, which everyone accepts as a breakfast item. If a fruit topping, such as the Strawberry Glaze (page 184), or *coulis* is added, its nutritional content becomes even more glorious.

½   *cup graham cracker crumbs*
1½ *pounds nonfat cream cheese*
      (3 8-ounce packages)
¾   *cup sugar*
1   *teaspoon vanilla extract*
3   *eggs*
2   *cups sliced fresh fruit (strawberries, mangos, peaches, plums, nectarines)*

■ Line each muffin tin with an aluminum cupcake liner. Spray liners with vegetable oil. Sprinkle cups with crumbs. In a large bowl using an electric mixer combine cream cheese, sugar, and vanilla. Beat in eggs one at a time. Pour into cups. Bake at 325° until the centers are set, 30 to 35 minutes. Refrigerate for several hours. Top with fresh fruit or other topping before serving.
Serves 12.

ROASTED GARLIC AND PARMESAN ASPARAGUS

In a busy restaurant it is sometimes easier just to put a vegetable in the oven and let it roast. Fresh asparagus, about a generous pound, is cooked in a covered dish with herbs, chopped garlic, and olive oil. When still crisp, freshly shredded Parmesan is sprinkled on top and browned in the oven. The asparagus should be al dente when served.

1¼ *pound asparagus, with tough bases removed*
1   *tablespoon olive oil*
1   *tablespoon dried Italian herb mix*
2   *cloves garlic, chopped*
½   *teaspoon black pepper*
¼   *cup shredded Parmesan cheese*

■ Place asparagus in a large ovenproof pan with a cover. In a small mixing bowl combine oil, herbs, garlic, and pepper. Pour the mixture over the asparagus and toss. Cover pan. Roast in a 400° oven for 10 to 12 minutes. Sprinkle with cheese. Return to oven uncovered for 2 minutes, or until the cheese is melted.
Serves 4.

VICTORIA ROWELL'S THAI SHRIMP SOUP

Add up to 1 additional tablespoon of Thai red chili paste for serious chili heads. Spicy chilies and soups are both good for satisfying hunger and keeping figures in shape. Jasmine white rice adds a wonderful fragrance to this dish.

2   cloves garlic, crushed
1   teaspoon oil
3   cups chicken stock
1   tablespoon Thai red chili paste (available at Oriental markets)
2   teaspoons soy sauce
1   tablespoon nam pla (fish sauce)
1   tablespoon minced ginger root
½   cup raw white rice
8   ounces shrimp, shelled and deveined
     Juice of 3 limes
     Sprigs of fresh cilantro for garnish

■ In a medium pan sauté garlic in oil for 2 minutes. Add chicken stock, chili paste, soy sauce, nam pla, ginger, and raw rice. Bring to a boil. Reduce heat and cover for 20 minutes. Add shrimp, heating until pink and warmed through, about 2 minutes. Stir in lime juice. Divide among soup plates. Garnish with fresh cilantro.
   Note: In Thailand this soup is made with kefir limes and a cousin of ginger called *galangal*.
Serves 4.

MICROWAVE POPCORN NEED NOT BE BORING

Possibly this is one of the easiest snacks for a quick crunch fix, but when the only choices are butter or not, it may not be exciting. Megan Dennison and her college friends have devised their own ways to add excitement to those bursting kernels. They also use the serious popcorn industry jargon "butterflies" as a classic popped kernel (never identical) and "bees' wings" for those little brown-yellow husks that get stuck in your teeth, but "old maids" for the unpopped kernels can send their fantasies into a spin.

1   bag microwave popcorn
     Seasonings—select one of the following combinations:
Italian: ½ teaspoon ground Italian herbs and 1 tablespoon grated Parmesan cheese
Southwestern: ½ teaspoon chili powder
Indian: ½ teaspoon curry powder, ¼ teaspoon ground cumin
French: ½ teaspoon herbs de Provence
Wisconsin: ¼ cup grated Wisconsin cheddar cheese
Cajun: ½ teaspoon ground Cajun spices
Chinese: ½ teaspoon Chinese five-spice powder
Cinnamon: ½ teaspoon ground cinnamon mixed with 1 tablespoon confectioners' sugar

■ Pop the corn following the package instructions. Carefully open the bag to avoid a steam burn. Add one of the seasoning combinations. Roll over the top to close and then shake.
Serves 2 or 3.

GREAT NORTHERN WHITE BEAN AND VEGETABLE SOUP

One of the marvelous joys of cooking is to be creative. With this vegetable soup there really are no rules. Experiment with the ingredients of the season, the contents of your pantry, and your whims. But be fore-warned: The Wisconsin folks always top this with grated cheese.

1	pound dried Great Northern beans
2	carrots, diced
2	ribs celery, diced
1	turnip, peeled, diced
2	cloves garlic, pressed
1	14-ounce can diced tomatoes in puree
1	bay leaf
2	yellow squash, sliced
1	pound fresh spinach, chopped (or substitute frozen spinach)
1	tablespoon salt
1	teaspoon pepper

■ Wash beans. Place in a pot and cover with 3 inches of water. Bring to a rolling boil. Cover. Turn off heat and let soak one hour. Drain off water. Add about 8 cups water to beans along with carrots, celery, turnip, garlic, tomatoes, and bay leaf. Cover. Simmer until beans begin to soften, about 1½ hours. Add additional water if needed. Add squash, spinach, salt, and pepper. Cook for 10 minutes. Remove bay leaf before serving.

Note: A meat bone can be added during the cooking of the beans if desired.

Do not turn up your nose at the lowly turnip. The bitterness is right under the skin. So remove a thick layer of the peel to reveal this little Cinderella root vegetable.

Note: A useful bit of bean trivia—the Great Northern bean, a white bean, is the dried seed of the mature green bean.
Serves 8.

RED- AND GREEN-LEAF LETTUCES WITH WARM GARLIC-SESAME CROUTONS

The success of this salad depends on the quality of the bread. Use day-old, dense, bakery or homemade breads such as the mixed-grain varieties for the best results.

1	head red-leaf lettuce, washed and spun
1	head green-leaf lettuce, washed and spun
¼	cup olive oil
2	cloves garlic, pressed
3	tablespoons sesame seeds
½	pound day-old, whole-grain bread, cubed
1	tablespoon mixed Italian herbs, crushed
1	teaspoon salt
½	teaspoon ground black pepper
¼	teaspoon cayenne pepper, optional
	Juice of 1 lemon

■ Tear lettuces into bite-sized pieces and place in a large salad bowl. In a large nonstick skillet heat oil. Sauté garlic and sesame seeds for 2 minutes. Add bread, herbs, salt, and peppers. Reduce heat to medium and toss ingredients (except the lettuces) in oil mixture. Stir occasionally and cook until bread begins to toast, about 15 minutes. Squeeze fresh lemon over greens. Cover with warm crouton mixture. Toss and serve immediately.
Serves 4 to 6.

SHEMAR MOORE'S STIR-FRIED BEEF, STRING BEANS, AND WATER CHESTNUTS

The most rigorous part of preparation for this stir-fry is slicing and chopping. Freeze beef for about 10 minutes for easier slicing. Slice mushrooms and scallions. Now most of the work is done. Stir-frying in a wok is fast as long as the oil is very, very hot. The resulting mixture, which coats the beef, forms a spicy sauce.

1   *pound boneless top round beef steak*
2   *tablespoons hoisin sauce (available in Oriental markets)*
2   *tablespoons soy sauce*
2   *tablespoons sherry*
1   *tablespoon cornstarch*
1   *teaspoon hot chili paste, optional*
2   *tablespoons peanut oil*
½   *pound string beans, cut into 1-inch pieces*
½   *pound mushrooms, sliced*
2   *scallions, sliced*
1   *8-ounce can sliced water chestnuts, drained*
2   *cups steamed rice*

■ Cut beef into ⅛-inch slices. In a glass dish such as a 10-inch pie pan, mix hoisin, soy, sherry, cornstarch, and optional chili paste. Add meat. Stir to completely coat meat. In a wok or large nonstick skillet heat oil on high until a drop of water dances on the surface. Stir-fry beans, mushrooms, scallions, and water chestnuts until tender, about 3 minutes. Push vegetable mixture to the top sides and stir-fry beef mixture until no longer pink inside, about 2 minutes. Mix vegetables, meat, and sauce. Place in serving dish. Serve with steamed rice.
Serves 4.

THE UNFRIED FRIES

Fat is out. Especially in Genoa City. These fries are wildly popular in January, when those after-the-holiday diets become the rage and all the Stairmasters in the health club are busy.

3   *large baking potatoes, scrubbed*
    Vegetable cooking spray
½   *teaspoon salt*

■ Microwave potatoes on high for 10 minutes or until they begin to soften. Cut each potato lengthwise into 8 strips. Place on a broiling pan with skin side down. Spray with vegetable cooking spray. Broil until the tops are browned and crisp. Salt and serve.
Serves 4.

RASPBERRY-ORANGE YOGURT ENERGY BOOST

Just slip all these ingredients into a blender and get ready for a healthy energy boost. When raspberries are out of season, substitute the frozen ones or some other luscious fruit such as papaya.

½   *pint fresh raspberries*
1½ *cups nonfat plain yogurt*
4   *tablespoons frozen orange*
      juice concentrate
1 to 2 *tablespoons sugar, optional*

■ Mix all ingredients in blender until smooth. Add optional sugar depending on desired sweetness.
Serves 2.

Lily

Dru was in the middle of a photo shoot when she suddenly went into labor. The photographer, her brother-in-law Malcolm, rushed her to the hospital. After she was admitted, Malcolm reached Dru's husband, Neil, who immediately raced to the hospital only to be thwarted by heavy traffic. Meanwhile, Dru sensed that something was wrong with her labor, and her doctor realized that the baby's life was in danger. Neil arrived in time to approve a cesarean section. Meanwhile, Malcolm withdrew to the hospital chapel to pray fervently for mother and child. As if in answer to his prayer, Dru gave birth to a healthy baby girl, whom she and Neil named Lily, after her mother. From that moment, Malcolm put aside any feelings he may once have had for Drucilla, realizing t hat her future and her happiness were with his brother Neil.

SOUTHWESTERN CHICKEN BURGERS WITH JALAPEÑO CHEESE BUNS

This burger packs a punch while waking up the taste buds. To be thematically correct, pass around plenty of tortilla chips with a chunky salsa. Be prepared with a jar of pickled jalapeño slices for those daring to be reckless.

> 1½ pounds freshly ground chicken
> 1   onion, chopped
> ¼   cup medium-hot chunky salsa
> 1   tablespoon chili powder
> 1   teaspoon salt
> 1   teaspoon black pepper
> 4   jalapeño cheese buns (substitute thick
>   slices of jalapeño cheese bread, the
>   following recipe)
> 1   avocado, sliced

■ With a fork gently combine chicken with onion, salsa, chili powder, salt, and pepper. Grill over medium hot coals for about 6 minutes on each side or until the meat is completely cooked. Place on grilled bun and garnish with avocado slices.

Note: If traditional burger buns are used, add a big slice of Monterey Jack cheese and jalapeño slices to each burger.

Makes 4 burgers.

CHEDDAR CHEESE AND JALAPEÑO CHILI PEPPER BREAD

Slices of this bread are good with the Southwestern Chicken Burgers or all by themselves. The bread freezes well. It also toasts well and makes a spectacular hit when grilled. A milder bread can be made with New Mexico-style chopped green chili peppers.

> 1   package dry yeast
> ¼   cup warm water, 105° to 115°
> 1   teaspoon sugar
> 3   cups flour
> ½   cup yellow cornmeal
> 1   teaspoon salt
> 1   cup milk
> 1   egg, beaten
> 6   ounces sharp cheddar cheese, chopped
> 1   4-ounce can chopped jalapeños or green
>   chilies, drained

■ Sprinkle yeast over warm water. Stir in sugar. Let sit 5 minutes until bubbly. In a large mixing bowl, mix flour, cornmeal, and salt. Stir in yeast mixture, milk, and egg. Knead with bread hook or by hand for 8 minutes. Knead in cheese and chilies. Put in a bowl. Cover with plastic wrap; let rise 1 hour or until doubled in size. Punch down dough. Transfer to a lightly floured pastry board. Form into 2 round loaves. Place on greased baking sheets. Let rise for 45 minutes. Bake at 350° for 35 to 40 minutes or until the top is golden.

Makes 2 small loaves.

TOASTED CAJUN-SPICED PEPITAS

Pepitas, or pumpkin seeds, purchased at the Genoa City Healthy Foods Emporium satisfy crunchy cravings. As an added benefit, these seeds pack 29 percent protein, more than most seeds.

1	*tablespoon vegetable oil*
1	*teaspoon Cajun spices*
¼	*teaspoon sugar*
¼	*teaspoon salt*
2	*cups pepitas (pumpkin seeds)*

■ In a medium skillet, heat oil. Stir in spices, sugar, and salt. With a spatula, toss pumpkin seeds until coated. Toast over low heat, stirring occasionally until crispy and puffed, about 10 minutes.
Makes 2 cups.

Nathan Jr.

Even though Nathan Hastings Jr. is only five years old, he has already faced great challenges in his young life. The untimely death of Nate's father, whom he adored, was a crushing blow for the boy. It appeared for a while that his grief would be insurmountable. The loving patience of his mother, the beautiful Dr. Olivia Hastings, was instrumental in helping the child to begin to cope with his tragic loss. It was not until she began to date and

ultimately married the dynamic Malcolm Winters that little Nate's life was once again complete. Malcolm became the stepfather who would help young Nate regain security in his world and rediscover the happiness that living each day can bring.

NANCY BRADLEY WIARD'S BARLEY SURPRISE

This is a great alternative to rice, pasta, or potatoes. "It's a recipe that came from my mother," says Nancy. "It goes great with chicken. I can make it the night before and serve it for dinner. It's also very good at elegant dinner parties."

1	*small onion, chopped*
1	*cup barley*
2	*tablespoons butter or olive oil*
3	*cups beef broth*
1	*7-ounce can sliced mushrooms, drained*
¼	*teaspoon freshly grated nutmeg (or substitute ground nutmeg)*

■ In a Dutch oven with a lid sauté onion and barley in butter or oil for 4 minutes, or until the barley begins to brown. Pour in beef broth, mushrooms, and nutmeg. Stir. Cover. Bake in 350° oven for about one hour, until the grains have absorbed all the liquid.
Serves 6.

Victor Jr.

Hope's pregnancy was filled with turmoil. From the beginning she and Victor were at odds. She wanted to stay on her Kansas farm before and after giving birth, and Victor was overly concerned that the child might be born blind—like his mother. Hopeless, Victor returned to Genoa City, convinced that she preferred staying at the farm in order to be close to her friend Cliff, who was recovering from a tractor accident. She was hospitalized after taking a tumble, and Victor rushed back and argued that she should return to the city with him, where she would be safe. She refused to accept his cold reprimand, and he chose not to stay once she appeared to be all right. His harsh words, however, had crushed her spirit, and Hope went into labor prematurely. When the doctor tried to call Victor, Hope asked him to call Cliff instead. After rushing to the hospital Cliff offered to contact Victor, but Hope insisted he wait until her labor pains were confirmed. Ignoring her wishes, he immediately phoned Victor, but the child was born while Victor was en route from Genoa City. She named the baby Victor Jr. but still refused to return with Victor to the city, believing that the farm was a healthier environment for her baby. Victor, however, returned to Genoa City and did not see his son for several weeks.

SABRYN GENET'S SEVEN-LAYER COOKIES

Sabryn Genet's (Tricia) advice for this fun cookie is "vary according to personal taste." The greatest effort required is to open all the packages. The base is a graham cracker crust mix. Then, going up the layers, are chocolate, butterscotch, walnuts, coconut, and sweetened condensed milk. The seventh layer must be the one that might start growing on your hips if you eat all of these glorious sweetnesses.

1   package graham cracker crumb mix with amount of butter and sugar as directed on package
1   small bag chocolate chips
1   small bag butterscotch chips
1   small bag chopped walnuts
1   small bag flaked coconut
1   small can sweetened condensed milk

■ Spray a 13x9-inch metal pan with vegetable oil. Following directions on the graham cracker crumb box, add butter and sugar. Press crust firmly down in the pan. Sprinkle on chocolate chips. Cover with butterscotch chips. Top with chopped walnuts. Top with coconut. Lightly cover with condensed milk. Bake at 350° until brown on top, 20 to 25 minutes. Cool completely. Cut into squares.

Note: If using a glass pan, lower heat to 325°. Watch for burning on the bottom.

Makes 36 squares.

Sharon poses with her infant son, Noah, and Cassie, a young girl she befriended without realizing she is the daughter she gave up for adoption.

GENOA CITY SAVORY AND CRUNCHY CREATIVITY MIX

There are those times when one needs something salty and crunchy, along with some substantial body. Find a market with one of the bulk bin systems of munchies. Grab some bags and scoop away. Let your creativity run rampant. Or make the mix right in the store—but only if each item is the same price.

2   cups cheese sesame sticks
1   cup shelled pistachios, toasted
1   cup sunflower seeds, toasted
1   cup thin mini-pretzels

■ Mix all ingredients together. Store in an air-tight container.
Makes 5 cups.

BITTERSWEET CHOCOLATE CHUNK MACADAMIA NUT BROWNIES

If the events of the day become just a bit too much or even overwhelming, there is nothing quite like this rich, chewy, blonde brownie studded with huge chunks of dark chocolate and macadamia nuts to divert attention to life's more pleasurable aspects. Traditionalists usually team these brownies with a glass of cold milk.

4   ounces butter, room temperature
1   cup packed brown sugar
1   egg
1   teaspoon vanilla extract
¾   cup flour
1   teaspoon baking powder
½   teaspoon salt
⅔   cup (about 4 ounces) semisweet chocolate squares, room temperature
½   cup macadamia nuts

■ With an electric mixer, cream butter and sugar until light and fluffy. Beat in egg and vanilla until fully incorporated. Add flour,

Nick and Sharon feel blessed to have their son, Noah, in their lives.

baking powder, and salt. Beat until well mixed. With a knife, cut chocolate into ¼-inch chunks. Stir in chocolate and nuts. Bake in a lightly greased 8-inch-square baking pan at 350° for about 25 minutes or until a knife inserted into the center comes out clean. Cool. Cut into 2-inch squares.

Makes 16 brownies.

PEANUT BUTTERY CHOCOLATE CHIP COOKIES

The comfort of old-fashioned peanut butter combined with the sensuality of chocolate makes this an irresistible cookie to share with someone you love or just to eat all alone to drown your distresses.

½	cup butter
1	cup sugar
⅔	cup old-fashioned peanut butter
1	tablespoon molasses
1	egg
2	tablespoons water
1⅔	cups flour
½	teaspoon baking soda
2	cups semisweet chocolate chips

■ In a medium mixing bowl, cream the butter and sugar until light and fluffy. Add peanut butter, molasses, egg, and water, stirring until completely incorporated. Mix in flour and baking soda. Mix in chocolate chips. Drop with a #40 scoop or a heaping tablespoon on a greased baking sheet. Bake at 375° for 12 minutes or until edges begin to brown. Cool for 2 minutes on the pan. Remove to cooling rack.

Makes 48 cookies.

Noah

Noah is a miracle baby in the fullest sense of the word. His mother, Sharon Newman, had taken a nasty fall during a severe snowstorm and was rushed to the hospital, where doctors initially worried that they would be able to save only one of the two lives involved. As Sharon was being prepared for surgery, she tearfully pleaded with Nick, her husband, not to let their baby die. Fortunately, both mother and child survived the procedure. The baby, meanwhile, was placed in a life-supporting incubator because his lungs were underdeveloped. A grateful Nick and Sharon saw that God had given them a wonderful gift, and so they gave their son a biblical name—Noah. Another crisis hit when Dr. Josh Landers, Nick's step-dad, detected that the baby's heart had stopped beating. Devastated, Nick and Sharon struggled to cope with the news. They rejoiced when the infant's heart began to beat again. Miraculously, the little guy was healthy enough to be released from the hospital a few weeks later.

Recipes for Singles

Everyone is single at some point, and sometimes it seems like the right person will never appear. Sometimes romance is elusive even when it seems to be all around. The singles of Genoa City know what it's like to eat alone, and some are tired of the easy fast-food route. They look instead for practical recipes that are easy to make and can also be prepared for more than one serving. Leftovers can be frozen or stored in the refrigerator, possibly even shared with a friend—but then they might want to turn to some of the more romantic recipes in another chapter.

HEARTY BEEF AND BARLEY ROOT VEGETABLE STEW

Lynne Basset often prepares this robust stew at home, saving a generous portion for her boss, Paul. She can heat this in the office microwave on the days he chooses to lunch at the office. Serve with a green salad and crusty bread.

2	pounds beef chuck steak, trimmed of all fat
¼	cup flour
2	tablespoons vegetable oil
2	large onions, chopped
2	cloves garlic
¼	cup pear barley
2	cups beef stock
4	parsnips, peeled, sliced
1	turnip, peeled, sliced
1	rutabaga, peeled, sliced
2	carrots, peeled, sliced

■ Cut meat into bite-sized pieces. Toss with flour. In a large pot heat oil. Sauté beef, onions and garlic for about 8 minutes or until the beef is browned. Add barley and stock. Simmer over low heat covered for 50 minutes. Add vegetables and cook for 30 minutes or until the vegetables are tender.
   Note: Add water if the stew becomes too dry.
Serves 6.

BRAISED HOT TURKEY SAUSAGE, RED POTATOES, AND SAUERKRAUT

This lean, little German-style bistro meal cooks in the skillet in less than 30 minutes.

1	tablespoon vegetable oil
1	pound hot turkey sausages (about 4 to the pound)
2	onions, sliced
1	pound red potatoes cut into 1-inch cubes
1	16-ounce can sauerkraut, drained
2	tablespoons brown sugar
2	tablespoons prepared country-style Dijon mustard
1	tablespoon caraway seeds
½	teaspoon salt
½	teaspoon coarsely ground black pepper
½	cup dark beer or water

■ In a large skillet heat oil. Sauté sausages until browned on all sides. Add onions and sauté several more minutes. Reduce heat to medium. Add potatoes. Stir and brown. Mix in sauerkraut, brown sugar, mustard, caraway seeds, salt, and pepper. Add water or beer. Cover and cook until sausages are no longer pink inside and the potatoes are tender, about 10 minutes.
Serves 4.

NEW ENGLAND FISHERMAN'S CHOWDER

Dr. Curt Costner, originally from Maine, has a passion for seafood chowders. This recipe is an old one from his village; he updated it by eliminating the fatty bacon and heavy cream. Canned minced clams and vegetables form the base. Chunky potatoes and milk make it thicker and richer. Just before serving, the fresh fish and shrimp are added.

1	tablespoon vegetable oil
2	cloves garlic
1	large onion, chopped
1	rib celery, chopped
6	½-ounce cans minced clams with liquid
3	potatoes, cubed
2	cups milk
1	cup water
1	teaspoon crushed, dried thyme
6	ounces firm white fish fillets
4	ounces shrimp (frozen are fine if defrosted)
1	teaspoon salt
½	teaspoon ground white pepper

■ In a soup pot sauté in oil the garlic and onion until translucent, about 5 minutes. Add celery, clams, potatoes, milk, water, and thyme. Simmer until the potatoes are tender, 30 to 40 minutes. Add fish and shrimp. Cook until seafood begins to turn opaque, about 3 minutes. Stir in salt and pepper. Serve piping hot.

Note: Remove the soup from the heat source soon after adding the fish and shrimp. The carry-over heat will finish their cooking.
Serves 6.

BAKED COLORFUL CORN TORTILLA CHIPS

For flavor variation, try white, yellow, blue, and red corn tortillas. The chips taste best warm from the oven but will keep in an airtight container for a munchy attack. For variety try dusting a small amount of ground cumin on tortillas before cutting the tortillas into wedges.

1	dozen corn tortillas—white, yellow, blue, or red
	Salt

■ On a cutting board stack several tortillas. With a large chef's knife cut into 6 wedges. Arrange on a baking sheet sprayed with vegetable oil. Spray pieces with more oil. Bake at 325° for 15 to 20 minutes until the chips begin to crisp. Salt. Store in an airtight container. *Makes about 60 chips.*

Lynne graciously placed aside her romantic feelings for her boss, private eye Paul Williams, when he married attorney Christine Blair.

PETER BERGMAN'S GRILLED HERBED CHICKEN

Marinate the chicken in a plastic bag then barbecue. It makes a real hit with children. Jack says, "The kids don't usually like saucings or toppings." This has lots of flavor without the undesired additions.

2	*pounds cut-up chicken parts*
½	*cup orange juice*
2	*tablespoons apple cider vinegar*
1	*tablespoon Dijon mustard*
1	*tablespoon chopped fresh basil*
1	*tablespoon chopped fresh rosemary*
1	*clove garlic, minced*
½	*teaspoon salt*

■ Place all ingredients in a closeable plastic bag. Marinate in the refrigerator for several hours turning the bag occasionally. Brush grill with vegetable oil. Remove chicken pieces from marinade. Grill 4 to 6 inches from medium hot coals or gas grill with dark meat over the highest heat. Grill white meat about 20 minutes and dark pieces about 35 minutes turning once. Chicken is done when it is no longer pink in the center.

Note: Substitute 1 teaspoon of dried herbs if necessary.

Serves 6.

Grace Turner

A childhood friend of Sharon Newman's, Grace breezed into Genoa City like a hurricane without warning and became intrigued with the lavish lifestyle of the Newmans. When Sharon's husband, Nick, helped Grace to get a job at his father's company, she became infatuated with him. When Sharon's son, Noah, was born and his condition was extremely critical, Grace gave up her job to find Cassie, the daughter sixteen-year-old Sharon had given up for adoption, and brought her back to Genoa City. By then Sharon had given birth, and the premature infant was stabilized. Later, while Grace was baby-sitting Noah, Nick, who had had too many drinks, found her in the nursery and made love to her, believing she was Sharon. When he realized what he had done, he confronted Grace and realized that her feelings for him were very serious. By this time Grace had secured a new position at Newman Enterprises, ensuring that Nick would see her every day. Her actions demonstrate that Grace is a strong woman with a specific agenda—and that agenda includes getting Nick Newman.

Esther Valentine

A longtime maid at the Chancellor estate, Esther has yet to meet her own valentine. She believed she had found true love with Tiny, a plumber, but he disappeared when Esther told him that she was pregnant. She gave birth to a daughter, whom she named Kate. Esther next fell in love with Norman Peterson, a confidence man who was more interested in the Chancellors' fortune than their maid. He invaded the Chancellor mansion one night to crack their safe, but the burglary was interrupted by Katherine's husband, Rex, whom Norman killed. He was later convicted of the murder, but Esther blamed herself and offered to resign. A grieving Katherine, however, understood that Norman had taken advantage of Esther and rejected her resignation. Although twice spurned, Esther still hopes to one day find a genuine, lasting romance.

WAFFLED SWISS CHEESE AND MUSTARD SANDWICH

Give that old waffle iron a new lease on usefulness. Especially good for sandwiches are ones with nonstick surfaces. No, do not flip to the grill side. Stay on the bumpy side to create cheese-melting crevices. Betty Arnold read this hint in a magazine and has been delighting Victor Jr. with these novelties ever since. Sometimes Victor requests a bit of peanut butter instead of the mustard—that's perfection at his age.

2	ounces Wisconsin Swiss cheese
1	tablespoon country-style Dijon mustard
2	slices multigrain bread

■ Plug in waffle iron and get it hot. Slice cheese to cover the bread. Spread bread with mustard. Slip cheese between the slices. When the iron is hot, spray with vegetable oil. Insert sandwich and wait until cheese is melted and the bread is bumpy and crisp.

Note: Peanut butter fans may wish to use that elixir of life instead of the mustard. And cheddar fans may certainly consider this a fair field for a grilled cheddar with the traditional Major Grey's chutney.

Serves 1.

BOBOLIS TOPPED WITH ITALIAN TURKEY SAUSAGE, ARTICHOKE HEARTS, SUN-DRIED TOMATOES, AND SMOKED GOUDA

Prebaked Bobolis (pizza crust) perfectly create fast gourmet-style pizzas. Italian turkey sausages are readily available nationwide in supermarkets. After piercing with a fork they can be quickly microwaved then sliced for lowfat pizza toppings. Match with a French Beaujolais and candlelight for a satisfying, easy dinner.

1   *Boboli baked pizza crust (about 16 ounces)*
½   *pound Italian turkey sausage, cooked and sliced*
1   *6-ounce jar artichoke hearts, drained*
⅓   *pound smoked Gouda cheese, sliced*
3   *tablespoons sun-dried tomatoes packed in olive oil*
2   *tablespoons chopped fresh basil*

■ Place pizza crust on a greased baking sheet. Arrange with turkey sausage slices, artichokes, cheese, and sun-dried tomatoes with oil. Sprinkle with basil. Bake at 350° until all ingredients are heated and the cheese is melted, 15 to 20 minutes. Slice.
Serves 3.

Gina Roma

As the owner of Gina's resturant, Gina Roma is highly regarded by the people of Genoa City. Her strongest qualities are the loyalty and love she has for her younger brother, Danny Romalotti. Growing up, they had no one but each other for support. Their mother was gone and their father, Rex Sterling, was serving a long prison sentence. Eventually, Rex won his release and renewed contact with his children. He eventually married Katherine Chancellor but was killed during a burglary at the Chancellor mansion. Gina and Danny were devastated. After a stint on Broadway, Danny returned to Genoa City with a baby son, Daniel. Gina was thrilled at becoming an aunt and doted affectionately over her nephew, but she was leery of Phyllis, the infant's mother, suspecting that she did not love Danny and had trapped him into marriage. When the truth finally came to light, Gina was there to ease Danny's anger over Phyllis's betrayal.

Miguel Rodriguez

A valued member of the Newman family, Miguel's job as houseman allows him to keep a watchful and discreet eye over everyone. Originally, Miguel worked specifically for Victor Newman. After Victor and Nikki divorced, Miguel stayed at the Newman ranch at Victor's request. He has watched over Victor and Nikki's children, Victoria and Nicholas, and seen them grow into young adulthood. His keen understanding of the Newmans is especially appreciated when a family member faces a emotional crisis. Miguel intuitively knows the perfect meal to prepare and the right words to say to help lift their faltering spirits!

VEGETARIAN FAJITAS

Fajitas were traditionally made using an inexpensive cut of beef, the skirt steak, along with vegetables wrapped in a flour tortilla. We have eliminated the meat and "beefed" this one up with lots of freshly sautéed vegetables and sided it with an assertive salsa. Serve the flour tortillas on the side so the fajitas can be built at the table. Otherwise the wrappers will become soggy. Soggy tortillas become quite a challenge—these fajitas are usually picked up and eaten out of hand.

1	tablespoon vegetable oil
2	cloves garlic
2	large onions, sliced
3	medium zucchini, sliced
3	summer squash, sliced
1	green pepper, seeded, sliced
3	ears of corn
	Juice of 1 lime
1	cup grated cheddar cheese
8	large flour tortillas
1	cup Salsa Fresca (page 101)

■ In a large skillet heat oil. Sauté garlic and onions until wilted. Add zucchini, summer squash, green pepper, and kernels sliced off the ears of corn. Sauté until crisp-tender, 7 to 10 minutes. Just before serving, squeeze lime juice over vegetables and sprinkle with cheese. Wrap tortillas in foil. Heat in a 375° oven for 10 minutes. After serving, have each person fill tortilla with vegetables, adding salsa at will.
Serves 4.

COUNTRY HAM AND OYSTER POOR BOY

Poach oysters in their own liquid. It takes several minutes for them to firm up. Teamed with paper-thin slices of salty southern country ham and tangy onions, these are the snacks that quickly become legends.

4	*hard-crusted, poor boy sandwich rolls or fresh baguettes*
1	*pint oysters, poached in their own liquid and drained*
8	*paper-thin slices country ham*
4	*thin slices red onion*

■ Slice rolls lengthwise and toast until golden under the broiler. Fill with oysters, ham, and onion. Serve warm.

Note: Equally delicious when oysters are roasted in their shells then shucked.
Serves 4.

Lynne Bassett

Paul William's longtime secretary, Lynne Bassett, is the type of employee every boss hopes to employ. She's loyal, discreet, and fastidious. Until Paul's marriage to Christine, Lynne dreamed her boss would one day fall in love with her. Her romantic hopes were further encouraged by Paul's mother, Mary, who constantly offered suggestions on how Lynne might win his heart. During a brief breakup between Paul and Christine, it looked as if there might be a chance for Lynne, but after a couple of dates he told her he thought it would be better if they remained friends. Always the trouper, heartbroken Lynne put on her best face as she struggled to accept reality. Her strong character has helped her to put her feelings for Paul aside and respect his marriage. She even helped arrange a bridal shower for Chris. Rather than wallow in self-pity, Lynne firmly believes she will one day meet the man of her dreams.

SMOKED TURKEY BREAST AND CRANBERRY CHUTNEY PINWHEELS

Square or rectangular slices of smoked turkey work best for this colorful pinwheel. Each is spread with the Cranberry Chutney enhanced with cream cheese. Little is sacrificed by using nonfat cream cheese. The pinwheels get larger using 2 turkey slices overlapped. Make these several days in advance for easy entertaining.

½ **pound smoked turkey breast, deli-sliced paper thin**

¼ **cup cranberry-apple chutney (page 69)**

4 **ounces cream cheese, room temperature**

■ On a piece of wax paper or plastic wrap, place 1 or 2 slices of turkey. With a fork, combine chutney and cream cheese. Spread meat with a thin layer of the chutney mixture. Using paper or plastic wrap, tightly roll lengthwise. Repeat process with remaining ingredients. Refrigerate for at least 2 hours. Slice into 1-inch pieces. Serve with cocktail picks or on crispy crackers.

Note: Also try this with Major Grey's Chutney or orange marmalade in place of the cranberry chutney.

If times are tough and funds are scarce, substitute "scam ham"—turkey ham. Just chunk it for dipping into the cranberry chutney mixture.

Serves 6 to 8.

Tony takes a protective interest in young Cassie, who does not know that Sharon is her real mother.

PETER BERGMAN'S CHICKEN THIGHS POACHED IN TARRAGON AND WHITE WINE

When made for children, it is fine to substitute stock or water for the wine. If desired, egg noodles can be added during the last 10 minutes.

12	chicken thighs, 3½ to 4 pounds
1	cup white wine
1	cup water
2	cloves garlic, peeled and crushed
1	onion, sliced
1	tablespoon dried tarragon, crushed
1	tablespoon black peppercorns
1	teaspoon salt
	Sprigs of fresh tarragon for garnish

■ Remove skin and visible fat from thighs. In a 3-quart pan bring wine, water, garlic, onion, tarragon, and peppercorns to a boil. Add chicken. Reduce heat to a simmer. Cover and poach until thighs are no longer pink inside, about 20 minutes. Uncover and cook about 10 minutes more to reduce the poaching liquid. Add salt. Pour liquid into a fat-separator cup. Let cool slightly. Pour off fat, return liquid to pan, and reheat. Garnish with fresh tarragon.

Note: If time permits, refrigerate chicken and cooking liquid separately until fat congeals. Remove fat. Reheat chicken and poaching liquid.
Serves 6.

CHEESE QUESADILLA WITH AVOCADO AND SALSA

Quesadillas are crispy Mexican sandwiches. Easy to prepare, they make a satisfying, filling, and spicy snack. While the flour tortilla crisps on the outside, the cheese (of course, from Wisconsin) melts into an awesome fusion with the creamy avocado.

4	medium flour tortillas
1	cup grated Monterey Jack cheese
½	avocado, peeled and chunked
4	tablespoons Salsa Fresca (page 101)
1	tablespoon chopped cilantro, optional

■ On a nonstick griddle sprayed with vegetable oil place 2 tortillas. Sprinkle with cheese and avocado. Place remaining tortillas on top. Cook until cheese begins to melt and the tortilla begins to crisp. Turn over. Cook until crisp. Cut each into 6 pieces. Serve with salsa sprinkled with optional cilantro.
Serves 2.

Sabryn Genet

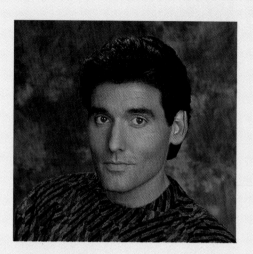

John Silva

A quick review of the *Genoa City Chronicle* archives would uncover several stories on dynamic attorney John Silva. While most of his clients are beautiful women in trouble, one of his most recent cases cleared Nicholas Newman of the shooting of Matt Clark, a former high-school football star. He has represented Christine Blair Williams in a rape case, defended April Lynch and Nina McNeil against murder charges, and waged Jill Foster Abbott's custody battle for her son, Billy. On at least two occasions Silva has been romantically involved with his clients. He briefly dated Nina, but their romance fizzled when she became involved with a young Jabot executive trainee. During Jill's custody battle, their passionate affair jeopardized his career and reputation. Realizing his position, Silva told Jill that he could be her lover or her lawyer but not both. Jill chose to retain him as her lawyer, probably a testimony to his legal skills but also a comment on his personal life.

FRESH TOMATO, RED ONION, SMOKED SALMON, AND DILL SPREAD WITH FLAT CRACKER BREAD

Savory snacking for some is the epitome of life. Heap the spread in a mound and surround by the giant, flat, crispy breads. Let everyone spread his or her own. To maintain the proper spread consistency, be sure to remove seeds and excess moisture from the tomato. This is also a sublime topping for bagels.

¼ *pound smoked salmon pieces*
½ *pound cream cheese, room temperature*
1 *large red-ripe tomato, skinned, seeded, finely chopped*
3 *tablespoons chopped red onion*
Juice of 1 lemon
1 *tablespoon freshly chopped dill*
1 *teaspoon salt*
2 *giant, flat cracker breads (such as Armenian)*

■ Chop salmon in small pieces. Cream salmon and cheese with a fork. Mix in tomato, onion, lemon juice, dill, and salt. Refrigerate until time to serve. Serve with flat cracker bread.
Serves 12.

CHUNKY SALSA FIXER-UPPER

Transform the supermarket's salsa into a lively tasting product by adding fresh ingredients. Most of these are available year round. Chop the tomatoes by hand, but not too fine. Take extreme caution in preparing the peppers, and keep your hands away from your eyes. If hand-burning does occur, rub your uhands with an acid such as lime juice. The desired result is a country-style salsa such as that prepared by Miguel Rodriguez's grandmother.

1   *8-ounce jar of salsa*
2   *ripe Roma tomatoes*
     Juice of 1 lime
2   *scallions, chopped*
2   *tablespoons freshly chopped cilantro*
1 to 2 *fresh jalapeño or serrano peppers,*
     seeded with interior ribs removed

■ Pour salsa into a rustic serving dish such as a terrific handmade piece of pottery. Coarsely chop the tomatoes. Gently add tomatoes and all remaining ingredients to serving dish. Do not refrigerate. Serve immediately.
Makes 1 1/3 cups.

Jack Abbott

Friends and foes alike know him as Smiling Jack for good reason: Jack Abbott can forge through any crisis and maintain a smile. Of course, when he's one-upping a rival or closing a multimillion-dollar deal for Newman Enterprises, his smile shines a little brighter. In business he's admired for his ability to size up all the angles and pick the best direction to take. Victor Newman demonstrated how much he values Jack's skills by asking him to help mentor his son, Nick, and Jack was more than happy to accept. When it comes to his family and friends, Jack is fiercely loyal. He cites his father, John, founder of Jabot Cosmetics, as his role model, and shares an exceptionally close relationship with his sisters, Ashley and Traci. A reformed playboy, Jack is single, but his relationships are extremely passionate. Always a gentleman, Jack takes the high road when a romance fizzles and maintains a friendly association with his past loves.

DOUG DAVIDSON'S RASPBERRY CHICKEN

4   chicken breasts, skinned
     and boned
2   tablespoons flour
½   teaspoon salt
3   tablespoons butter
1   shallot, chopped
1   cup chicken broth
1   tablespoon Chambord
     (raspberry liqueur)
2   tablespoons raspberry vinegar
½   cup heavy cream
     Red food coloring, optional
     Fresh raspberries for garnish

■ Remove all visible fat from chicken. Lightly coat with flour and salt. In a large skillet sauté chicken until browned, about 5 minutes. Turn over and finish cooking, about 5 minutes. Do not overcook. Remove chicken from skillet and keep warm. Sauté shallots in pan drippings until soft, about 2 minutes. Reduce heat. Add chicken broth, Chambord, and raspberry vinegar. Reduce by half over low heat. Stir in heavy cream and heat. If desired add optional red food coloring. Spoon sauce over chicken. Garnish with fresh raspberries.
Serves 4.

CRISPY BACON, FRESH SPINACH, AND TOMATO PITA SANDWICHES

Not many of the Genoa City folks are fooled—this is the trendy version of the old BLT. But they order it faithfully at the coffee shop because it tastes fabulous and the ingredients are fairly healthy.

2   whole-wheat pita pocket breads, cut to
     form hemispheres
4   slices crisp bacon, crumbled
1   bunch fresh spinach, cleaned, cut into
     narrow strips
2   large tomatoes, chopped
1   tablespoon Dijon mustard
1   tablespoon nonfat plain yogurt

Heather Tom

■ Gently open the pita bread hemispheres. Fill each pita with bacon, spinach, and tomatoes. Drizzle with a dressing made from stirring together the mustard and yogurt.

Note: The shop makes a vegetarian alternative of this sandwich by substituting texturized vegetable protein "bacon" bits.

Serves 2.

CAPPUCCINO AND VANILLA SWIRLED PUDDING

Keep this a secret. This dessert is ready in an instant with a little packaged help, but it looks terrific when you serve it in glass goblets. Most coffee shops sell the chocolate-covered coffee beans.

1   *package instant vanilla pudding*
2   *cups cold milk*
2   *teaspoons instant espresso, powdered (do not use freeze-dried granules)*
4   *chocolate-covered coffee beans for garnish*

■ In a mixing bowl beat instant pudding with cold milk for 3 minutes. Transfer ⅓ of the pudding to another small bowl. Mix in instant coffee. Divide vanilla pudding into 4 dishes. Add ¼ of the coffee pudding to each dish with a tablespoon. Using a knife blade, swirl coffee pudding into the vanilla. Chill. Before serving, top each with a chocolate-covered coffee bean.

Serves 4.

BROWN SUGAR AND BANANA ICE CREAM SUNDAE

The banana just lightly cooked in a buttery brown sauce is a perfect ice cream topper. The sauce may also be made in the microwave. Use a large glass dish to prevent the butter from splattering.

2   *tablespoons butter*
2   *tablespoons brown sugar*
1   *banana, peeled and sliced*
1   *tablespoon dark rum or 1 tablespoon orange juice*
4   *scoops of vanilla ice cream, frozen hard*

■ In a small skillet melt the butter with the brown sugar. Stir in the banana and cook for 2 minutes. Add rum or orange juice and cook 2 more minutes. Let cool slightly. Pour over scoops of vanilla ice cream.

Serves 2.

Scott Reeves

Just Desserts

There are villains, and then there are villains. Whatever their designs may be—revenge, riches, or just general wrongdoing—they all get justice eventually. Plots, conspiracies, and calories combine to create seemingly no-win scenarios, but the tantalizing dessert recipes found in this chapter are so good they're almost criminal!

WARM APPLE PECAN COMPOTE WITH CINNAMON ICE CREAM

The cooking aroma of the apples fills a home with love, and the taste of this dessert will solidify that love.

1	*quart low-fat vanilla ice cream*
1	*tablespoon ground cinnamon*
4	*tart apples, peeled, chunked*
¼	*cup sugar*
¼	*cup apple juice*
1	*teaspoon cinnamon*
½	*cup chopped pecans*
1	*teaspoon vanilla extract*

■ Allow ice cream to soften for about 5 minutes at room temperature. With a large, strong spoon swirl in cinnamon. Return to freezer to harden. In a medium saucepan bring apples, sugar, apple juice, and cinnamon to a boil. Reduce heat. Cook until the apples are just beginning to soften and the sauce starts to thicken, about 10 minutes. Remove from heat. Stir in pecans and vanilla extract. Cool for a few minutes. Serve in dessert cups topped generously with the cinnamon ice cream.
Serves 6.

INDIVIDUAL SUMMER FRESH FRUIT TRIFLE

This is a fresh fruit variation on the English masterpiece made monumentally in a straight-sided glass bowl to regally display the layers. In Genoa City, where things are usually somewhat more casual, this version takes advantage of our fresh summer fruits and convenience products.

8	*golden sponge cake dessert cups, sliced in half horizontally*
½	*cup sherry*
1	*cup vanilla custard*
2	*cups sliced peaches, plums, and berries*
¼	*cup slivered almonds, toasted*
1	*cup heavy cream, whipped*
2	*tablespoons confectioners' sugar*
½	*teaspoon vanilla*

■ Place bottom of each dessert sponge cake on individual plates. Sprinkle with sherry. Cover with vanilla custard. Top with fruits, saving a few choice pieces for top garnishes. Sprinkle with almonds. Place top of dessert cups on fruit and slather with whipped cream. Garnish with reserved fruits. Refrigerate.

Note: In a hurry? Use a mix of instant vanilla pudding for the custard and a ready-made whipped cream or low-calorie frozen substitute.
Serves 8.

BERN BENNETT'S HOLIDAY PUMPKIN CHEESECAKE

Bern Bennett has been the announcer for *The Young and the Restless* since the show began in 1973. Once a week Bern brings a supply of delicious baked goods he has made himself to the office for everyone to enjoy. This pumpkin cheesecake is impressive and delicious. It will freeze quite well if tightly wrapped.

CRUST
1½   *cups very finely crushed graham crackers*
¼   *cup sugar*
4   *tablespoons butter or margarine, melted*

FILLING
3   *8-ounce packages cream cheese,*
     room temperature
1½   *teaspoon vanilla*
1   *14-ounce can sweetened condensed milk*
3   *tablespoons flour*
4   *eggs*
1   *16-ounce can pumpkin*
1   *teaspoon cinnamon*
1   *teaspoon pumpkin pie spice*
½   *teaspoon ginger*
½   *teaspoon nutmeg*
     Whipped topping for garnish

■ In a medium bowl combine crushed graham crackers, sugar, and butter or margarine. Treat a 9-inch springform pan with vegetable spray. Press crumb mixture on the bottom and up the sides of the pan. In a large mixing bowl using an electric mixer gradually beat cream cheese, vanilla, and flour. Scrape sides. Add eggs 1 at a time until incorporated. Mix in pumpkin and spices until fully combined. Pour into crust.

Bake at 300° for 70 to 75 minutes, until center is set. Turn off the oven. Leave door ajar. Let cake cool to room temperature to prevent cracking. Remove from oven. Run knife around the interior edge of the pan. Chill cake for a minimum of 4 hours. Remove from pan. Serve with a dollop of whipped cream.
Makes 1 (9-inch) cheesecake.

APPLE HAZELNUT FRANGELICA PIE

This is a nutty apple pie with the fragrant taste of Frangelica. It is made with the tart, juicy apples grown right on Katherine Chancellor's estate. Often, thin slices are served to guests at teatime.

     Unbaked pastry for two-crust 9-inch pie
6   *cups sliced cooking apples*
     (about 2 pounds)
1   *cup sliced hazelnuts*
⅔   *cup sugar*
2   *tablespoons flour*
1   *teaspoon cinnamon*
1   *tablespoon Frangelica*
1   *tablespoon butter, cut in small pieces*

■ Line a 9-inch pie pan with bottom crust. In a bowl mix together apples, hazelnuts, sugar, flour, cinnamon, and Frangelica. Fill piecrust. Dot with butter. Cover with top crust. Cut slits in top crust. Bake at 425° for 10 minutes. Reduce heat to 350° and bake 45 to 55 more minutes until the interior is bubbly.
Makes 1 (9-inch) pie.

BLACKBERRY- AND RICOTTA-FILLED TARTS

This is a showy dessert relatively low in calories and fat. Make individual tart shells by cutting phyllo dough sheets into squares and layering them in muffin tins or small ramekins.

1   *7-ounce package frozen blackberries*
½   *cup sugar, divided use*
1   *cup low-fat ricotta*
1   *egg*
1   *tablespoon cornstarch*
1   *teaspoon vanilla extract*
2   *sheets of phyllo dough, 14x18-inch, about 3½ ounces, defrosted*

■ Sprinkle berries with ¼ cup sugar while still frozen to maintain their integrity. Let defrost at room temperature. Mix remaining ¼ cup sugar with ricotta, egg, cornstarch, and vanilla. Spray each sheet of dough with vegetable oil. Place 1 sheet on top of the other on a pastry board. Cut into quarters. Cut each quarter into 2 pieces. Line 6-ounce ramekins with 2 pieces arranged at 90° angles. Fold dough ends around the ramekin edges. Fill with cheese filling. Spoon blackberries on top. Bake at 375° for 15 minutes. Serve either warm or refrigerated.

Note: For cholesterol avoiders, this works beautifully with only the egg white. And for those wanting a richer item, use butter to layer the dough and whole-milk ricotta. *Serves 4.*

Michael Baldwin

Charismatic lawyer Michael Baldwin exploited his charm to hide the fact that he was a sexual predator. Newly licensed lawyer Christine Blair discovered the truth about his chilling personality after accepting a position with a prestigious law firm where Baldwin worked as her boss. He promised to aid her advancement in the firm in exchange for sexual favors. Christine filed a sexual harassment suit, prompting Baldwin to launch his own sinister campaign to smear her reputation. When Christine ultimately won her case, he tried to kill her. Fortunately, private eye Paul Williams arrived in the nick of time and shot Baldwin, who recovered from his wound and was sentenced to a lengthy prison term. Since then Baldwin has won his parole and returned to Genoa City, where Christine continues to be a source of consternation in his life.

BODACIOUS BLUEBERRY PIE WITH WHIPPED CREAM

There is really nothing more summery than a blueberry pie. Especially worthy of comment are the giant blueberries from Michigan. Thanks to modern technology, this pie can be enjoyed year around.

1	unbaked 9-inch pie crust
3½	cups blueberries, fresh or frozen
⅔	cup sugar
2	tablespoons flour
1	teaspoon lemon extract
¼	teaspoon nutmeg
1	cup freshly made whipped cream

Paralegal Michael Baldwin protected Phyllis with expert counsel when Danny filed for divorce. Meanwhile, Danny's legal interestests were protected by Christine.

■ Line a 9-inch pie pan with unbaked crust. In a bowl mix together blueberries, sugar, flour, lemon extract, and nutmeg. Fill pie. Bake at 400° for 30 to 40 minutes. Let cool slightly. Serve with generous dollops of whipped cream.

Note: Frozen blueberries need not be defrosted before baking. Extend baking time slightly. If crust becomes too brown, cover with strips of aluminum foil.

Makes 1 (9-inch) pie.

GREENGAGE PLUM CRUMBLE

This is one of those quick, everyday desserts that everyone loves. It makes a typical day nicer and helps everyone get his or her daily serving of fruit. Top with vanilla ice cream or frozen yogurt.

4	cups sliced, greengage plums
¼	cup brown sugar
2	tablespoons orange juice
2	tablespoons butter, melted
2	tablespoons brown sugar
⅓	cup flour
⅓	cup oat bran
½	teaspoon ground allspice
½	teaspoon salt

■ Toss plums with brown sugar and orange juice. Spray a 9-inch pie plate with vegetable oil. Fill with fruit mixture. In a small bowl combine with a fork the melted butter, sugar, flour, oat bran, allspice, and salt. Crumble over the fruit. Bake at 350° for 30 to 40 minutes or until the fruit becomes tender and the crumble begins to brown. Serve warm.

Serves 6.

MANGO LEMON SORBET

On those hot, muggy days of summer, this is a marvelous pick-me-up. Small portions also make a refreshing between-course palate cleanser.

2   *cups water*
¾   *cup sugar*
     Juice of 2 lemons
2   *ripe mangoes*
     Fresh mint sprigs for garnish

■ Bring water and sugar to a boil, stirring until dissolved. Stir in lemon juice. Cool. Puree mangoes in a food processor. Mix in sugar water. Pour into a small ice cream or sorbet maker. Follow manufacturer's instructions to make the ice. Scoop into chilled glass dishes. Garnish with fresh mint.
Serves 6.

David Kimball

In a plot to inherit the Chancellor fortune, David Kimball married Nina Webster and then planned to kill her and her son, Phillip. Previously, Kimball had used a different identity to marry and murder wealthy Rebecca Harper. His secretary, Diane, who was having an affair with him, discovered his past and joined him in his plot against Nina. Meanwhile, Nina's close friend, Chris, who didn't trust Kimball, obtained evidence linking him to his previous identity. After Nina overheard Kimball and Diane's plotting to kill her, Nina shot him. Kimball survived but pretended to be paralyzed. Nina was charged with attempted murder, but with Chris's help, she was acquitted. Angered, Kimball staged his own death and then assumed another identity, pretending to be Jim Adams, a southern aristocrat. As Adams he romanced and married Nina's mother, Flo, to keep tabs on Nina. Soon after, Kimball attended a masquerade ball and wore a wolf's costume. Nina, Chris, and Danny were also guests, and Kimball tried without success to kill the three. The bullets in his gun were made of wax. With private eye Paul Williams and the police in hot pursuit, Kimball/Adams took refuge in what he thought was a closet. Instead, it turned out to be a garbage chute, and he met a grisly death in a trash compactor.

MARITA DELEON'S LOW-FAT CARROT CAKE

This just proves that you can have your cake and eat it too and still stay healthful and slim. The cake is moist, even without fat, due to the carrots and pineapple. Without any egg yolks, it is totally cholesterol free. Use ½ cup juice reserved from draining the crushed pineapple. Grate carrots with a food processor for easier preparation.

1	cup crushed pineapple, drained
½	cup pineapple juice
½	cup light molasses
2	egg whites
2	teaspoons vanilla
4	cups grated carrots
1	cup flour
1	cup whole-wheat flour
2	teaspoons ground cinnamon
½	teaspoon baking soda
¼	teaspoon salt
	Dusting of confectioners' sugar

■ In a large mixing bowl stir together pineapple, pineapple juice, molasses, egg whites, and vanilla. In another mixing bowl combine flours, cinnamon, baking soda, and salt. Quickly stir dry ingredients into wet ones. Pour into a 9x13-inch pan sprayed with vegetable oil. Bake at 375° until a cake tester comes out clean, about 45 minutes. When cool, dust lightly with confectioners' sugar.

Note: Place a paper doily on top of the cooled cake. Dust with confectioners' sugar. Remove doily, creating a classic design.

Makes 1 (9x13-inch) cake.

Clint Radisson

When Clint Radisson proposed marriage to Gina Romalotti, she quickly accepted. Sadly, Clint, a former cellmate of Gina's father, Rex Sterling, had an ulterior motive. Marrying Gina was part of an elaborate scheme to get his hands on the Chancellor fortune. With the help of two thugs, Clint kidnapped Katherine and then arranged for Marge, a hash-slinging waitress who bore a remarkable resemblance to Katherine, to impersonate Katherine. Unfortunately for Clint, the kidnapping was bungled and the thugs also abducted Katherine's longtime maid, Esther. Complicating matters even more, Esther was very much pregnant. When she suddenly went into labor, Esther was taken to a hospital, where she managed to expose the scheme to Katherine's son, Brock, who persuaded Marge to reveal Katherine's whereabouts. Clint and his cohorts were arrested. Eventually, Clint escaped from prison and found refuge with Gina, who agreed to run away with him. Before they could start a new life together, Clint saved Brock's life and was called a hero. Afterward, he gave himself up to the police and returned to prison.

RICH CHOCOLATE FUDGE SAUCE

Just a bit of a chewiness results when this sauce hits ice cream, truly one of the magic combinations for late-night snackers. You might as well double this recipe, especially since it reheats beautifully.

3   *tablespoons butter*
5   *tablespoons cocoa*
1   *cup sugar*
1   *cup water*
2   *tablespoons corn syrup*

Jack and Diane vacationing at Saint Thomas. Later Jack gave up Diane when he rediscovered Luan, his teenage sweetheart.

■ Melt butter in a heavy-bottomed sauce pan. Whisk in cocoa and sugar. Whisk in water and corn syrup. Bring to a boil. Reduce heat to medium. Cook, stirring occasionally, for 6 to 8 minutes until the sauce is slightly thickened.
Makes 1 cup.

NOT-QUITE-SO-RICH CHOCOLATE FUDGE SAUCE

If you are watching cholesterol and fat grams, this is a more user-friendly fudge sauce for ice cream.

6   *tablespoons cocoa*
2   *tablespoons nonfat dry milk granules*
1   *cup sugar*
1   *cup water*
2   *tablespoons corn syrup*

■ In a heavy-bottomed sauce pan mix together cocoa, milk granules, and sugar. Whisk in cold water and corn syrup. Bring to a boil. Reduce heat to medium. Cook, stirring occasionally, for 6 to 8 minutes, until the sauce is slightly thickened.
Makes 1 cup.

STRAWBERRY GLAZE

Extraordinary desserts can be made by adding a fancy glaze. This one can top a cheesecake, Breakfast Cheesecake (page 151), or fresh strawberries in a pie.

10 **ounces frozen strawberries**
3 **tablespoons sugar**
1 **tablespoon cornstarch**
3 **tablespoons orange juice**

■ Place strawberries and sugar in a saucepan. Bring to a boil. Cook for 3 minutes. Dissolve cornstarch in orange juice. Stir into strawberry mixture. Bring to a boil constantly stirring. Reduce heat and cook until clear, about 2 minutes. Cool.
Makes 1 1/2 cups.

Mari Jo Mason

Mari Jo was on the verge of marrying Jack Abbott when his son, Keemo, sent an urgent fax to Jack's boss, Victor Newman, imploring him to protect his father from Mari Jo. Keemo had been romantically involved with her, but she had ended that relationship to pursue Jack. Victor confronted Mari Jo with the fax and advised her to keep away from Jack, adding that the fax was hidden in a safe place. Soon after, while Victor was involved in a late-night meeting with attorney Christine Blair, Victor was shot. Christine was unable to identify the assailant. After Victor recovered, he hired private eye Paul Williams to find the would-be killer, but in the end, Victor solved the mystery himself. He realized that Mari Jo's alibi was a lie. After he confronted Mari Jo, she kidnapped Christine. During a physical struggle with Mari Jo, Christine managed to knock her kidnapper to the ground and escape. As Mari Jo ran after Christine, Victor and Paul arrived. Soon after, Mari Jo was committed to a mental institution.

APRICOT-AND-BRANDY-GLAZED SPICE CAKE

This one-bowl, no-mixer cake stirs up fast. The glaze of brandy and dried apricots goes on while the cake is still hot, giving the appearance of an elegant, rich pastry, but its richness is in the flavor, not the fat.

CAKE
1	egg
½	cup vegetable oil
⅔	cup milk
⅔	cup sugar
1	teaspoon vanilla extract
1½	cups flour
1	teaspoon baking powder
1	teaspoon ground cinnamon
1	teaspoon ground allspice
1	teaspoon ground nutmeg
½	teaspoon ground cloves
½	teaspoon salt

GLAZE
½	cup dried apricots, chopped
¼	cup water
¼	cup brandy
¼	cup sugar

■ In a medium bowl whisk egg, oil, milk, sugar, and vanilla. Add flour, baking powder, spices, and salt. Stir until just incorporated. Pour into a greased 9-inch round cake pan. Bake at 350° for 25 minutes or until a knife inserted in the center comes out clean. Cook apricots, water, brandy, and sugar in a small saucepan over medium low heat for 10 minutes or until slightly thickened. Spoon glaze over cake while still warm.

Note: Substitute 2 egg whites for the whole egg for a cholesterol-free cake.

Makes 1 (9-inch) cake.

ICE CREAM BROWNIE CREPE WITH CHOCOLATE FUDGE SAUCE

Fill the crepes with chocolate fudge ice cream for a triple-chocolate treat, or use vanilla bean ice cream for a brilliant contrast. The crepes can be made ahead and frozen, if desired.

1	cup flour
3	tablespoons confectioners' sugar
2	tablespoons cocoa powder
½	teaspoon baking soda
¼	teaspoon salt
2	eggs, beaten
1	cup milk
2	tablespoons water, optional
1	pint chocolate fudge ice cream (or substitute vanilla bean ice cream) *Rich Chocolate Fudge Sauce (page 183) or Not-Quite-So-Rich Chocolate Fudge Sauce (page 183)*

■ In a small mixing bowl, combine flour, sugar, cocoa, soda, and salt. Quickly mix in eggs and milk. Batter should be very thin. If too thick, add optional water. Heat a small skillet or crepe pan. Spray with vegetable spray. When medium hot, pour about ⅓ cup batter into the pan so that it just covers the bottom after spreading. Cook until browning begins on the bottom, about 1 or 2 minutes. Flip over and finish cooking. Repeat procedure for each crepe, spraying pan with vegetable oil between each crepe. To assemble, fill crepes with ice cream. Top with fudge sauce.

Serves 6.

INDEX